Existential Authenticity

Jonathan Davidov • Pninit Russo-Netzer

Existential Authenticity

Theory and Practice

palgrave
macmillan

Jonathan Davidov
University of Haifa
Haifa, Israel

Pninit Russo-Netzer
Achva Academic College
University of Haifa
Haifa, Israel

ISBN 978-3-031-07841-5 ISBN 978-3-031-07842-2 (eBook)
https://doi.org/10.1007/978-3-031-07842-2

This Palgrave Macmillan imprint is published by the registered company Springer Nature Switzerland AG.
The registered company address is: Gewerbestrasse 11, 6330 Cham, Switzerland

Acknowledgements

We wish to acknowledge and thank all those who advised, contributed, helped, and consulted to the research and writing of this book.

First we would like to thank the 'Compass' institute for research, development and application of meaning in life, and all the members of the board who contributed to the modification and updating of the theory.

We also would like to thank our students who, over the years, assisted in collecting data and most importantly experienced the approach and commented and contributed to the fine tuning of the model of existential authenticity.

We also wish to thank Daphna Goren and Rachel Alberg who contributed to the data analysis and provided insightful comments throughout the process.

A special thanks to Dr. Tomer Fekete who read, commented, and helped to make our ideas much better articulated.

We also wish to thank our graphic designer Nadia Davidov who contributed her images to illustrate the central ideas in the book.

Finally, we wish to express our deepest gratitude and appreciation to our families who supported us in the long journey of working on this book in our search for existential authenticity.

We hope this book will accompany anyone who seeks self-discovery and growth, and aspires to live a more fulfilling and meaningful life.

Contents

List of Figures

List of Tables

Introduction

This book focuses on the idea of existential authenticity in theory and in practice. It introduces core principles on the one hand and practical knowledge for everyday use on the other. Existential questions have always been a part of human life since the dawn of its existence, but in the current era of economic and material prosperity, technology and social networks, questions of meaning, freedom, and authenticity emerge more forcefully with regard to individual and social order.

This book follows Søren Kierkegaard's (2013) definition of authenticity as recognizing that which is meaningful to a person, and its practical application in his life. This idea is elaborated through Kierkegaard's understanding of Abraham's binding act of Isaac in the book of Genesis in the Bible. According to Kierkegaard, Abraham experienced his encounter with God in an authentic, subjective, and personal way. Consequently, he couldn't explain the binding act (namely his plan to take his only son to the mountain of Moriah, to sacrifice him to God) to his wife Sarah and others around him in an objective and logical way. The binding is a non-rational act which contradicts reasonable moral values, and therefore cannot be explained in a rational way. However, for Abraham it is a very meaningful act demonstrating his authentic bonding with God. Authenticity, thus, is a different state of mind that complements and is even sometimes opposite to rational thinking, in which one expresses and follows in his life what is meaningful for him, much like following a compass that directs one to an unknown but meaningful destination. Such a state of mind takes both courage and deliberate intention, and it is not achieved in an automatic manner. When modified, it can act as a balancing force that adds and complements logic and rationality, and as such, be an essential tool to achieve well-being in human life.

It can be argued, generally, that the current era, characterized by the fast-paced development of technology, requires an expression of authenticity, uniqueness and originality. Processes such as globalization, the crumbling of individual and social identity in various dimensions including communities and social frameworks such as families, tradition, and growing secularism, intensify questions of authenticity ('who am I, really') and meaning in life ('why am I here and what do I value'). It is similar to the way in which the agricultural era required physical strength in order to face the demands of farming the land. Another parallel can be seen in the necessity brought on by the industrial era for rational and logical thinking which were essential in order to face the engineering challenges of developing machines for production, and for understanding the rules and principles which underline the industry and the economy.

In fact, the technological era sterilized and weakened the need for rational thinking. Nowadays, the calculating capacities of computers can replace that type of thinking with growing efficiency, and humans are required to demonstrate additional abilities beyond relying on rationality. They are challenged to re-invent themselves in additional arenas. Individuals need to prove that they possess uniqueness and exceptionality beyond the logical and rational capacities they were expected to adopt in the past. Now they are required to become 'authentic humans', who bring their own unique and meaningful added value into the collective reality.

Furthermore, in the current post-modern, global, and digital age, in the face of crumbling traditions and religious structures, and in the absence of anchoring principles, uncertainty, instability, alienation, and loss of meaning are ever present (Moules 2000). Research from the last few decades consistently indicates a significant rise in levels of anxiety and depression despite a considerable rise in economic prosperity and the standard of living (Diener & Seligman, 2004; Twenge, 2000). The recent outbreak of COVID-19 pandemic further intensified these processes and invoked a wide range of crises worldwide. Social distancing, uncertainty, isolation, and anxiety led to a rise in mental distress and phenomena such as addiction, stress, a sense of existential vacuum, alienation, depression, and suicidality (see, for example, Czeisler et al. 2020). More than ever, humanity is confronted with essential personal and social questions—How do we find meaning in our lives? How can we live our lives in a more meaningful way?

At the same time, and despite the recent increasing need for such ability of 'being authentic', there are no available concrete and practical tools that can help us understand and discover our authenticity—as individuals or as a collective. This book deals with this pressing need.

The book is based on original scientific research as well as classic literature in the field of existential thought. It aims to draw for its readers a conceptual map to allow them to better navigate their day-to-day experiences. Based on the existential perspective, the main axiom of this book is that people are 'thrown' into a complex existential human condition which involves a great extent of vulnerability on the one hand, and possibilities to live a full and meaningful life on the other hand.

In this book, we redefine human beings as meaning-seeking entities. We point out the immense powers that are engrained in us alongside our vulnerability, finiteness, and isolation that we are challenged to endure as humans. This framework paves the way towards the main argument of this book, namely, that it is the authentic, direct and experience-based interaction with our vulnerability and existential anxiety that is the key to unleashing our potential for change in both our personal and external realities. The book aims to provide a sort of 'manual' for such an experience-based encounter—an encounter which aims to increase the sense of freedom and meaning in the day-to-day human experience.

The book is divided into two parts. The first part presents the main principles of existential thinking, its perception of human consciousness, its limits, and possibilities. The second part suggests a practical approach to existential therapy, and focuses on the human authentic experience and how it can be used to facilitate change in a person's behavior and self-perception.

Each of these parts is a standalone unit so that those interested in learning more about the theoretical principles of existential thinking may find the first part informative. The second part is more practical, offering a concrete framework for implementing existential thought in day-to-day life, and in therapeutic settings in particular. As such, the book can also serve as a guide for self-use in order to practice the principles of existential authenticity in one's life.

References

Czeisler, M. É., Lane, R. I., Petrosky, E., Wiley, J. F., Christensen, A., Njai, R., & Rajaratnam, S. M. (2020, June 24–30). Mental health, substance use, and suicidal ideation during the COVID-19 pandemic—United States. *Morbidity and Mortality Weekly Report*, *69*(32), 1049.

Diener, E., & Seligman, M. E. (2004). Beyond money: Toward an economy of well-being. *Psychological Science in the Public Interest*, *5*(1), 1–31.

Kierkegaard, S. (2013). *Fear and trembling and the sickness unto death.* Princeton University Press.

Moules, N. J. (2000). Postmodernism and the sacred: Reclaiming connection in our greater-than-human worlds. *Journal of Marital and Family Therapy*, *26*(2), 229–240.

Twenge, J. M. (2000). The age of anxiety? The birth cohort change in anxiety and neuroticism, 1952–1993. *Journal of personality and social psychology*, *79*(6), 1007.

PART I

The Main Principles of Existential Thinking

CHAPTER 1

'Everything Is Foreseen, and Permission Is Granted'

Abstract The goal of this chapter is to explain the concept of social reality as co-constructed—how our choices shape and influence the way we experience our lives and our relationships with other people—and to understand humans' freedom and responsibility for their lives from an existential perspective. It includes an introduction to the theory and main concepts of existential thought and discusses the Sartrean approach to free will and the possibility of freedom of choice as a central concept in human psychology.

Keywords Existential philosophy • Kierkegaard • Nietzsche • Sartre • The myth of Oedipus • The concept of Death and mortality • The concept of Freedom and responsibility • The concept of free will

Existential philosophy was first introduced to the world in the nineteenth century. Logic and rationality in Western culture were leading values, with the blooming dominance of science and positivism. This was also the era of the industry and the machine, and its far-reaching influences on all areas of human life: family, society, culture, and religious practices. The main philosophical conception of human existence at the time was similar to a natural system, ruled by nature law. It was seen as managed by a set of clear rules that can be defined in an accurate and deterministic way.

J. Davidov, P. Russo-Netzer, *Existential Authenticity*,
https://doi.org/10.1007/978-3-031-07842-2_1

Georg Hegel, the leading philosopher of that time, phrased this perspective well by stating that humans are passive subjects, controlled and ruled by the 'Zeitgeist'—the laws of human history that predict and frame the course of social and cultural development (Hegel, 2018).

The counter movement to this emphasis on pure rationalism was the Existential movement, born toward the end of the nineteenth century, and led by European intellectuals such as Kierkegaard, Nietzsche, and others. Those thinkers were alarmed by the industrial revolution and the rational thinking which characterized modern science. They were startled by the damage they believed it caused to the fabric of human living and especially to the loss of the sense of freedom and meaning—a loss leading, eventually, to an experience of existential vacuum and despair. Their main argument was that understanding humans as whole beings should not be narrowed to merely their rational existence.

The first to rise to the challenge was the mid-nineteenth century Danish thinker Søren Kierkegaard who addressed two forms of human existence: the ethical and the aesthetic. The aesthetic form of existence derives from the external world as a response to the social and cultural demands of the environment surrounding the individual. This way of life corresponds with Hegelian rationalism, being governed by external rules (Kierkegaard, 2013).

The other form of existence, the ethical one, is created by an intimate encounter between an individual and their internal world which is personal and subjective, and therefore not subjected to an external set of rules. This is also an authentic way of living, and it is expressed by the way in which an individual opts to view reality and to interpret the 'facts' of their surrounding society.

Therefore, the social and cultural 'facts' (the zeitgeist) are subject to interpretation, and each individual may understand them somewhat differently. A gigantic struggle takes place in every individual's mind between their rational or aesthetic parts and the authentic, subjective parts. The struggle manifests itself in the experience of the absurd, which comprises the gap between rationality and authenticity (Kierkegaard, 2013).

Kierkegaard argues that even the most rational human being, living the most normative life and well-adjusted to social norms, occasionally encounters the absurd—a clash between the rational and social norms with an internal force that desires something different. The less an individual follows their authentic and subjective voice, the more they may sink into an empty and meaningless existence. Meaning involves the ability of giving expression to the authentic and spontaneous aspects of human nature. We will further expend on the notion of Kierkegaard's 'absurd' and its relation to meaning in Chap. 3.

The importance of meaning and authenticity to human life is further discussed by mid-nineteenth century philosopher Friedrich Nietzsche, who pointed out the nihilism and absence of meaning that lie at the core of scientific-rational thinking. Nietzsche pointed out that an individual may find meaning by engaging life from a subjective and personal perspective, which he dabbed as 'the will to power' (Nietzsche, 2005). That is to say, self fulfillment can be achieved by intentional and personal confrontation with reality, and not by 'surrendering' to the orders of logic and nature. In this sense, humans are not like seeds, which inevitably turn into the plants that exist within them as a potential (a rationalistic-determinist approach); rather, they are a project based on subjective will, and they can turn into everything that they intend to become.

These ideas set the foundations for Husserl's phenomenology, which evolved in the first half of the twentieth century, based on the presumption that the real meaning of phenomena is not as relevant to the understanding of human nature, as the meaning which an individual attributes to it in their subjective consciousness (Husserl, 2012). During the twentieth century those ideas evolved into existential philosophy and psychology, known through the works of martin Heidegger (Heidegger, 1962), Jean-Paul Sartre (Sartre, 1956), Viktor Frankl (1963), Irwin Yalom (Yalom, 1980), and many others.

Its main argument is that only an authentic and direct encounter with reality, namely experience-based rather than an intellectual/logical encounter, can keep existential vacuum and despair that accompanies it at bay. Despite all this progress, ever since its introduction in the nineteenth century (see Kierkegaard, 2013; Nietzsche, 2005), Existential thinking gained only a rather limited hold in comparison with other schools of modern psychology—the Psychodynamic and the cognitive-behavioral. This might have to do with its more philosophical vocabulary or due to its limited practical research anchoring concrete protocols for intervention, and evaluation processes.

'Everything Is Foreseen'—The Human Destiny

One of the main principles of existential thought refers to human condition of mortality and freedom. In order to understand this position, and especially human mortality concept, it may be useful to embark on re-reading one of the core myths of Psychodynamic psychology, the myth of Oedipus (Hanscomb, 2006).

This myth, although mostly known in relation to the psychodynamic approach, is also highly relevant to Existential thought, offering a somewhat different interpretation.

Oedipus was the son of the king and queen of the city of Thebes. Upon his birth, a prophecy predicted that he was destined to kill his father and marry his mother. In an attempt to avoid fate, the king of Thebes ordered to kill his son as soon as he was born.

The soldier who was ordered to carry out the king's decree had felt that his heart did not allow him to do so; therefore he traveled to a faraway land and gave Oedipus for adoption to a poor couple of peasants, and they raised him. The peasants had sworn not to let Oedipus know his true identity; so, he grew up oblivious to his real parentage. He believed his adoptive parents were his biological parents.

Oedipus grew to be a diligent young man. One day he came across a fortune teller who told him he has to kill his father and marry his mother. Oedipus was horrified, as he did not want to harm his beloved parents. To avoid the harsh prophecy, he parted with his parents and embarked on a journey to a faraway land, where the prophecy could not materialize.

While on his way, a disturbing event occurred to Oedipus. He was strolling along the main road, when suddenly a rich man in a carriage emerged riding in the middle of the road and scolded all other foot-travelers to make way for him.

Oedipus felt that the stranger's behavior was malicious and enraging, and he refused to move aside and let the carriage pass. A conflict developed, during which Oedipus ended up killing the nobleman who was driving the carriage. What Oedipus did not know then, was that the rude nobleman was none other than his father, king of Thebes. Half the prophecy, then, was already fulfilled: Oedipus had killed his own father.

Oedipus went on his way and reached the outskirts of Thebes. In those days, the city was maligned by the Sphinx monster that blocked the way to the city and demanded that every traveler would solve its riddle, or die. In fact, it subjected the city to a siege, under which no one could get in or go out. In their plight, the residents, who had recently lost their king, swore that whoever removed the siege and dealt successfully with the blockading monster—would get to marry the queen and inherit the kingdom.

Oedipus knew none of this. He arrived in the city after a long journey, and found himself facing the Sphinx, who presented him with her riddle: "What walks on four feet in the morning, two in the afternoon and three at night?" Oedipus knew the answer instantly: A person as a baby in the morning of their life crawls on four feet; as an adult at the noon of their life, they walk on two feet; and when they are old, in the evening of their life, they walk with a cane, on three feet. Upon hearing the answer, the Sphinx evaporated, and Oedipus received an honor he did not expect: he was invited into the city as a hero to marry the queen and inherit a big fortune. Thus, of course, the prophecy was fulfilled in its fullness: he killed his father and married his mother.

So goes the myth; from here on, the interpretations vary. The classic psychodynamic interpretation views it as a developmental stage in an individual's personality. This is considered the phallic stage, the third stage of psychosexual development, characterized by the 'Oedipus Complex', when the infant male, only familiar with his own family circle, aspires to overcome his father and conquer his mother as a spouse in his stead.

At the heart of this developmental stage is the self-worth of the developing young person in the context of a competition over limited resources. Upon successful completion of this developmental stage, there will be a personal acknowledgment of the infant's own self-worth, alongside exiting the family circle and realizing that there are other potential women, apart from his own mother, who can become his spouse. Thus, the competition against the father is resolved, and the young person is relieved from the complex and can get on with his life. At this stage, a youngster's sense of self-worth crystalizes, equipping him to deal with future challenges in the reality of his life. It should be noted that women also go through the same stage, known as the 'Electra complex', in which the roles are reversed, but the essence remains similar.

The Existential approach offers a different, possibly more 'natural', interpretation for the myth, which does not relate to 'developmental stages'. Rather, the narrative evolves around the idea of human destiny, according to which every individual has a fate that they cannot escape, no matter what they do, or how far they try to escape from it, fate is destined to prevail. Oedipus was destined to kill his father and marry his mother, and no matter how hard he tried to escape this certain fate, it caught up with him.

Therefore, the main issue here is acknowledging and dealing with human destiny as the force that structures human behavior, rather than the competition against the father and the desire to conquer the mother. In other words, the main premise which molds human behavior does not lie in the dynamic of one's childhood, rather in the human condition, and primarily in being mortal and conscious of this fact. This issue cannot be reduced or explained away by other psychological factors, but should be considered for its own sake. As Heidegger (1962) suggests, humans can't avoid the factuality of death and finality that is sure to come, and much of their behavior is influenced and revolved around this subject, especially in a negative way of being anxious and fearing this destiny, and doing everything possible to avoid it.

A moment of thought: where do you experience your mortality in your life?

- Note, this does not refer to an objective or intellectual notion of mortality, but your own personal experience of mortality and perhaps vulnerability in your life.

Alongside one's potential destiny, which is reflected in the "all is known" (the finality of death) aspect of existence, there is also an additional aspect of "permission is given"—encapsulated in the fact that humans are free to choose their own interpretation of their life and the way they react to it. The following part explains this matter, as well as why humans are often challenged by their freedom and may invest much effort in escaping it.

"Permission Is Granted"—Humans Are Destined to Be Free

In a poignant article entitled "Existentialism is Humanism", French philosopher Jean-Paul Sartre (see Sartre, 2007) presents an intellectual exercise that helps illuminate the idea of human freedom and points out to its implications for human behavior and experience. Let's begin by exploring this exercise in a free manner yet true to the original framework. Then, we shall discuss its implications on the human condition of freedom and self-perception.

Sartre tells the story of a young French man at the age of conscription, during World War II, who faces a heart-breaking dilemma: on the one hand, the war is at the country's doorstep, there is a decree for mandatory conscription, and all the young men of his age are off to the frontline to fight, risking their lives in defending their homeland. On the other hand, this specific young man faces an unusual predicament: his elderly mother is in a poor health condition and needs constant care. Nobody else can, in the existing circumstances, take it upon themselves to provide it for her. The mother will not last long without the needed care.

The young man, therefore, faces a quandary: on the one hand is his moral commitment to the collective and to the defense of his country, and putting them before those of the individual, in order to preserve society. Obviously, if everybody were to put their personal needs before those of the collective—society will not survive. Without the collective, individuals cannot survive. In other words—without France, the mother would die anyway.

On the other hand, there is the young man's commitment to his mother and family, and the importance of personal morality. Going to war and defending the whole nation relate to a general value, the outcomes of which are not clear; the young man might die, and the homeland might not survive, in which case his sacrifice would be in vain in national/political terms. But as far as his personal and more immediate goal goes, it is clear that staying by his mother's side would tip the balance between her survival and her death, in favor of the former. Here, the significance is clear and more concrete. How does one choose between two conflicting values, between collective morality and individual one? How does one choose between a nation and a mother?

Our young man is very ethical, and he wants to find a true and honest answer to the question—one that would maintain his integrity. He wants to know which value is more meaningful, more important. He assumes that a hierarchy of values does exist, and that a wise man knows how to discern and run his life astutely, in accordance with high ideals. He therefore seeks a clear answer to his predicament.

First, our young man turns to the Holy Scripture, the bible, and its later interpretations, dealing with morals and right and wrong norms of behavior since antiquity. He is convinced that the answers will be found there.

But he soon realizes that reality is more complex than anticipated. The Holy Scripture's guidelines for moral life are general, and not easily adjustable to the unique reality of every human being. For example, Christianity recommends that when in a moral dilemma one should opt for the more challenging and harder way (Sartre, 2007).

Which, therefore, is the hardest way in this case? Is it choosing to take care for the mother or opting for the war? Everybody may agree that a war is a hard path to take: it involves a bare and direct contact with the powers of nature, there is a possibility of facing hunger, distress, aggression, physical and mental pain, and to a great extent a likelihood of violent death. It is, indeed, a hard path.

But what about caring for the ailing mother—Changing her diapers, feeding her, brushing her teeth, bathing her? Obviously—a physical danger for the life of the caregiver is not involved, or at least, the level of danger is no different than the normative state of things. However, the direct encounter with helplessness, decline, finality and all they entail, is not to be taken lightly. It is even possible that for young people, fighting at the frontline is 'easier' than nursing the elderly and seeing them in their most exposed way imaginable.

Such perspective which offers general guidance can also be found in other religions. For example in Judaism it is a central value that one should go to war when the homeland is threatened. However, there are exceptions in Jewish law ('Halacha') recognizing 'special conditions'. For instance, young men in the first year of their marriage are exempt from military service. This opens the door for a discussion regarding 'special situations'—which is exactly where we stand. Does nursing an ailing mother come before going to war? The Jewish Scripture has no concrete answer.

Having failed to find an answer in the Holy Scriptures and traditions, the French youngster turns to secular wisdom, as reflected in the writings of the philosophers of morality. Here he finds Immanuel Kant and his extensive book about morality (Kant, 2017). The scope of this book is not wide enough to describe the depth of Kant's work, and the various debates about morals which it invokes. But if we choose but one central sentence from the book, we should focus on the general idea that 'moral behavior is this that views others as an end in itself and not as a means to something else'. The importance of this moral imperative is that if one wants to treat their fellow human morally, one must address them as a purpose in their own rights, and not as a means to get their own objectives.

Kant's noble idea turned into a practical criterion in various contexts and moral dilemmas. It constitutes, in general, a central idea in secular moral thinking of our time (either as a guideline for conduct or as a subject for criticism). And yet, despite its importance, the principle remains too wide and general for our young Frenchman, as it still does not spell out who has precedence: the mother or the nation? In other words:

1. Is the mother the purpose of morality, in which case the nation is a means to secure her safety? In such a case the young man should stay with his mother and protect her.
2. Is the nation the purpose of morality, and then the mother's welfare is only secondary to this superior goal? If this is the case—then the young man must go and defend the nation.

We are, then, back to square one, and we still are no closer to saving the young man from his agonizing dilemma. Having failed to find the answer in religion and in philosophy, the young man turns to the route of feelings and emotions and to his instincts and intuition. Maybe here lies the answer? Maybe he should find the solution in listening to the voice of his inner emotion? Maybe he will discover that he prefers to go to war, and follow this sentiment, or he might realize that he prefers to protect his keen in the first place, and act accordingly. Namely, the answer is deep inside his own soul, and he only needs to find it there. But here, too, we must ask, is there a more basic emotional condition? Are there 'more important' and 'less important' emotions to lead our day-to-day life?

To respond to the young man's questions, it may be worthwhile to take a closer look on the nature of emotions. What are they? And here is an unequivocal answer—an emotion is essentially a mental and physical condition which always appears in an intersubjective context, relating to an individual's interpretation of their given situation. In other words, it depends on context and does not stand in its own right.

Take, for example, the following situation: you are driving your car, listening to the radio, and feeling wonderful. You are in no hurry, the day is sunny, and you let yourself drift into a pleasant ponder about your life. Suddenly, another car emerges from behind you, overtakes you wildly, and nearly gets you into an accident. This is the event you have experienced. Now, you have a few options.

You may think "what a delinquent and impudent driver!"; this reading of your situation could lead you toward an angry emotion, and maybe even a defiant response like chasing the wild driver and attempting to catch up with him at the next traffic light and "teach them a lesson". On the other hand, you might think, "maybe the driver is in distress? Maybe the driver's spouse is sick? Maybe the driver is in a hurry to get to a hospital?" This interpretation could lead to a very different, compassionate emotion, and maybe to a different behavior, aiming to help the driver progress toward their destination.

The following diagram illustrates this state of affairs (Fig. 1.1).

Back to our Frenchman, he realizes that whatever he feels is a result of his interpretation of reality; therefore, the emotion does not precede the decision and rules over it, but the other way around—the emotion is an outcome of the interpretation. Therefore, emotion is not the right instrument for making the moral decision he seeks, between personal and collective moral. What is left for him to do?

The young man decides that his dilemma is too big to be dealt with on his own, and he seeks an expert advisor. If religion and philosophy do not have the specific answers for his unique situation but only general guidelines, and if emotions are strictly context dependent—maybe an advisor could save him from his predicament.

But a problem arises here, too: an advisor cannot be just anybody, but only a person who other people 'consider' to be wise and expert. Such

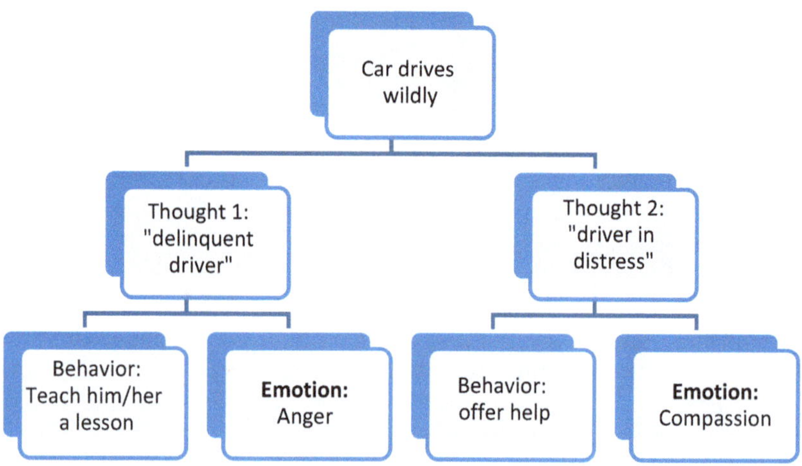

Fig. 1.1 The connection between emotion and interpretation

people, thought to be wise, are also 'known' and accepted as such by the general public. Therefore, the advisor's orientation can be predicted before the young man even turn to them, and the spirit of their answer could be expected.

For example, if we turn to a university professor who is known, in certain circles, to be wise, we are likely to encounter an individualistic intellectual moral orientation; if we turn to a religious scholar, who is also reputed to be wise among a different sector of the public, we are likely to receive a more collectivistic, community-related moral approach. Therefore, choosing a specific advisor is very much akin to picking a possible answer; and again, the young man will never know whether the answer is definite, or just based on the advisor's own inclination.

In his distress, the young man turns to reflect on his existential condition only to realize that humans are destined to be free! There is no beacon that can lead him to 'right' or 'wrong' behavior. According to the Existential approach, humans are 'orphans' at crucial points of their lives with no clear guidance and no stable ground under their feet. This is the sense of groundlessness that characterizes our human freedom. No one can tell us what is right and what is wrong—not the scriptures nor philosophy, not science nor our emotions. The attempt to rule on moral dilemmas using scientific or religious tools is, in fact, an attempt to escape our existential condition, where responsibility for all its weight lays upon us alone.

In other words, there is no 'right' choice for the young Frenchman. He is the one that must make this critical choice that will affect the manner in which his future life will unfold, and if he wants to be true to himself, he should not blame someone or something else, such as God or science, for his choices. Whether he decides to stay with his mother or go to war—it is his choice. And to maintain his integrity (which was the main motivation for his quest) he will explain to himself that he is doing what any person in his situation would have done. Most importantly, this means that the realization of the young man's belief system and guiding principles are shaped after he made his choices, not prior to it.

Our belief system is therefore 'ex-post-facto'—it is shaped after we make our existential choices, and is influenced by them. That is to say, in order to maintain integrity, free individuals are compelled to shape their guiding principals after making choices and based on those choices, as in "my way is the moral way". The following chart describes the choices made by the young Frenchman and the shaping of his belief system (see Fig. 1.2).

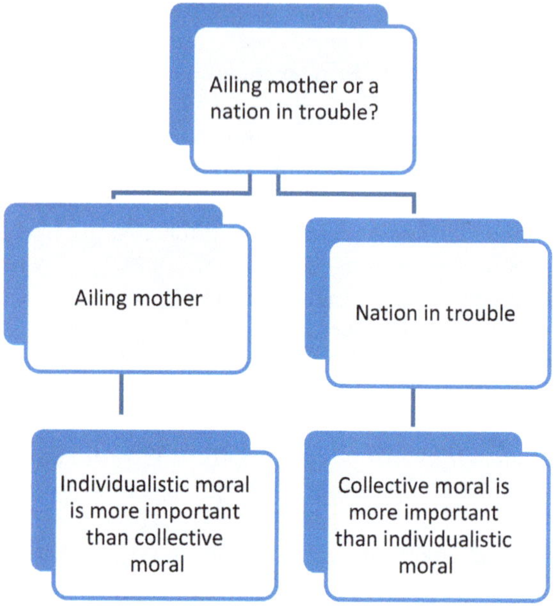

Fig. 1.2 Materializing belief system as an outcome of choices made

Hence, humans have the very compelling power to shape their worldview and the way they interpret and experience the reality of their life at any given moment. They alone decide, at a given circumstance and social context, what is good and right in their reality, and what is bad and damaging in it. They can change that choice at any given moment and thereby alter their experience, their reality, and the way they live in the world, perceive it, and understand it.

This does not apply only to crucial decisions between going to war and nursing a sick mother, but also to daily choices that characterize routine situations: should I give money to a beggar in the street? Should I be tough on my child or opt to be soft and understanding in this instant? Should I speak or keep quiet during a staff meeting at work? Each of these decisions requires a choice between two options or more. And with each choice, we face our situational freedom, namely, the freedom existing in given circumstances and the ability to make a change from one moment to the next in our perception of ourselves and our world. In this sense, every person fully co-creates their lived experience, because they can decide how to live in a given reality and experience it. This is a very remarkable and invaluable power.

The idea of free will was discussed at length in many studies. There is a consensus regarding 'free will' as one of the most important ground concepts of Western culture, upon which its ideas of justice are based (Smilansky, 2002). At the same time, there is a long controversy involving the key question whether free will and free choice exist at all, and if so, to what extent. On the one end, there are those who argue that free choice is an illusion, that everything that happens is inevitable, and that no other scenarios are possible (Crick, 1994; Smilansky, 2000, 2002; Wegner, 2002). On the other end are those who claim that life gives us choices, and that those who tell themselves that they had no alternatives, in fact use self-delusion in order to escape the consequences of their choices on their life and on their self-identity (Baumeister, 2008; Sartre, 2007).

This philosophic dispute has no clear-cut solution, and there are valuable arguments on both sides of the divide. However, it has significant implications on human psychology, which is also the concern of this book. In fact, the belief in free will largely influence the way individuals treat others socially. In general, studies demonstrate that those who reject the ideas of free choice tend to display anti-social thinking and behavior, including aggression and unwillingness to help others (Baumeister et al., 2009), avoiding creative and independent thinking, and reluctance to change and to learn from past experiences (Alquist et al., 2013; Stillman & Baumeister, 2010). At the same time, belief in free choice is related to more adjustability and flexibility in social relations and the propensity for creative and independent expression (Leotti et al., 2010; Stillman & Baumeister, 2010).

A previous study examined whether the experience of freedom of choice remained valid even in extreme situations such as for prisoners in Nazi concentration camps (Davidov & Eisikovits, 2015). The study discovered that the human experience of choice is maintained even in such radical conditions and is almost never extinguishable. In other words, as long as people experience themselves as a human being, they experience situational freedom even within total institutions aiming to extinguish such experiences. However, once the choice is eliminated, the individual's sense of self and agency is negated alongside their capability to communicate with their environment.

In the context of Nazi concentration camp, such an individual with no free will was turned into a 'Musselman'—with no experience of a 'self' or any will, a living-dead creature who simply kept existing until the Nazis executed them (Davidov, 2015; Davidov & Eisikovits, 2015). In conclusion, even if the question of the existence of free will is unconcluded philosophically, cognitively, physiologically, or neurologically—it can be said that phenomenologically, in terms of the human experience, free choice exists as an essential element of the human existence. Eliminating it would lead to an extinguishing of the human subjective experience of 'self' as an agent, leading an individual to a self-alienation and withdrawal from life.

It is important to highlight a few significant implications regarding the freedom of choice and the ability to decide how to experience reality. Those are related to the reason for the human reluctance to encounter freedom, and the desire to escape it as much as possible (see Fromm, 1942). First, a free individual would always feel **existential guilt**, because nothing stopped them from making a different choice. If the young Frenchman opts to go to war, his mother's death would always burden his conscience. And if he chooses to stay at home, he would feel guilty for the deaths of his friends.

Choice invokes guilt even regarding more mundane decisions: opting to be tough on a child means compromising their innocence; being soft implies infringing on their independent development and ability to endure frustration. Opting to speak in front of the whole class involves self-exposure, and subjecting oneself to possible criticism over the opinions expressed. However, keeping silent suggests leaving the stage to others, and avoiding self-expression—another cause for guilt.

Free individuals, therefore, are doomed to feel guilty, because they can blame nobody else for their condition: not science, nor God or circumstances. The human individuals alone made the choice to behave as they did under given circumstances, and this guilt is hard to bear.

Second, the other facet of guilt is the responsibility implied by freedom and by the ability to choose how to live. When individuals realize that only they can choose how to structure their own world, they also assume responsibility for all that they perceive as good or bad in their reality. That is to say, existential freedom involves a responsibility for how people experience their reality; therefore, the experience of existential freedom goes hand in hand with a deep sense of responsibility for the way we live. Or, in the words of Victor Frankl (The Doctor and the Soul, 1986, p. 76):

> *Being human is being responsible because it is being free. It is a state of being that—as Jasper says—first decides what it is. It is 'deciding being'; it is 'existence'. The table in front of me is and remains what it is, at least for its part, that is to say—unless a human being puts a hand to it and changes it. But the human being, who sits across from me at this table, decides in every case who he 'is' during the next second, what he will say to me, or conceal from me. There is a multitude of different possibilities in his being, of which he actualizes only one, and in so doing determines his existence as such. During no moment of his life does a man escape the mandate to choose among possibilities. Yet he may pretend to act 'as if' he had no choice and n freedom of decision. This 'acting as if' if' constitutes a part of the human tragicomedy.*

Taken together it can be suggested that the human experience of freedom is a collection of burdening factors that invoke existential anxiety. They motivate humans to escape the experience of their own freedom. As Frankl notes, they may pretend 'as if' they have no real choice or freedom to make decisions. In Sartre's words, they may sink into self-deception and self-delusion (see Sartre, 2007), which diminishes them into victims of reality rather than partners in establishing it. This is what Frankl means by referring to the tragi-comic essence of human life.

In summary, existential thinking postulates human mortality and freedom as a part of human reality, and as a central element of Human's way of being in the world. This postulation of free will facilitates two main basic positions toward it—accepting it or denying it. Accepting freedom with all it entails is considered an authentic experience of existence, while denying it is seen as a non-authentic experience. We will examine authenticity in depth in the following chapters; but first, we will focus on the subjective experience of freedom for itself and look into what can be learned from it.

References

Alquist, J., Ainsworth, S., & Baumeister, R. (2013). Determined to conform: Disbelief in free will increases conformity. *Journal of Experimental Social Psychology, 49*(1), 80–86.

Baumeister, R. (2008). Free will in scientific psychology. *Perspectives on Psychological Science, 3*, 14–19.

Baumeister, R. F., Masicampo, E. J., & DeWall, C. N. (2009). Prosocial benefits of feeling free: Disbelief in free will increases aggression and reduces helpfulness. *Personality and Social Psychology Bulletin, 35*, 260–268.

Crick, F. (1994). *The astonishing hypothesis: The scientific search for the soul.* Simon & Schuster.
Davidov, J. (2015). *Identity, self and free will in total institutions.* Lambert academic publishing.
Davidov, J., & Eisikovits, Z. (2015). Free will in Total institutions—The case of Choice in Nazi death camps. *Consciousness and Cognition, 34,* 87–97.
Frankl, V. (1949/1963). *Man's search for meaning: An introduction to logotherapy.* Pocket Books.
Frankl, V. (1949/1986). *The doctor and the soul: From psychotherapy to logotherapy.* Second Vintage Books.
Fromm, E. (1942). *The fear of freedom.* Routledge.
Hanscomb, S. (2006). Contemporary existentialist tendencies in psychology. In *Phenomenology and psychological science* (pp. 169–196). Springer.
Hegel, G. W. F. (2018). *Hegel: The phenomenology of spirit.* Oxford University Press.
Heidegger, M. (1962). *Being and time* (J. Macquarrie & E. Robinson, trans.) Blackwell.
Husserl, E. (2012). *Ideas: General introduction to pure phenomenology.* Routledge.
Kant, I. (2017). *Kant: The metaphysics of morals.* Cambridge University Press.
Kierkegaard, S. (2013). *Fear and trembling and the sickness unto death.* Princeton University Press.
Leotti, L. A., Iyengar, S. S., & Ochsner, K. N. (2010). Born to choose: The origins and value of the need for control. *Trends in Cognitive Sciences, 14,* 457–463.
Nietzsche, F. W. (2005). *Thus spoke Zarathustra: A book for everyone and nobody.* Oxford University Press.
Sartre, J. P. (2007). *Existentialism is a humanism* (C. Macomber, Trans.). Yale University Press.
Sartre, J.-P. (1956). *Being and nothingness: An essay in phenomenological ontology* (H. E. Barnes, Trans.). Philosophical Library.
Smilansky, S. (2000). *Free will and illusion.* Oxford University Press.
Smilansky, S. (2002). Free will, fundamental dualism, and the centrality of illusion. In R. Kane (Ed.), *The Oxford handbook of free will* (pp. 489–505). Oxford Press.
Stillman, T. F., & Baumeister, R. F. (2010). Guilty, free, and wise: Determinism and psychopathy diminish learning from negative emotions. *Journal of Experimental Social Psychology, 46,* 951–960.
Wegner, D. M. (2002). *The illusion of conscious will.* MIT Press.
Yalom, I. D. (1980). *Existential psychotherapy.* Basic Books.

CHAPTER 2

"Being Here", Dasein, and the Four Lifeworld Existential Modes of Subjective Experience

Abstract In this chapter we explore the components and structure of human consciousness, including cognitive mechanisms of rationality and processing patterns on the one hand, and the subjective experience of sensations, feelings, and emotions (i.e. lived experience), on the other. The chapter considers the components of the subjective experience from the perspective of hermeneutic phenomenology, according to which, each subjective (or lived) experience is constructed from the four lifeworld existentials of temporality (lived time), corporeality/embodiment (lived body), relationality (lived human relations), and spatiality (lived space). It introduces the concept of Dasein, which is the mediating factor between one's cognitive conceptualization of experience and the manner in which those experiences are subjectively lived through.

Keywords Subjective experience • Lived experience • Heidegger • Dasein • Hermeneutic phenomenology • Lifeworld existentials • Temporality • Corporality/embodiment • Relationality • Spatiality

In order to understand the subjective experience of freedom, which is a central concept, constituting the base point for Existential thinking and the psychology that derives from it, we will take a close look at the condition of the young Frenchman, before he chose whether to stay with his

J. Davidov, P. Russo-Netzer, *Existential Authenticity*, https://doi.org/10.1007/978-3-031-07842-2_2

mother or go to war. He is, in fact, in a state of existence in which it is still unclear how he should opt to exist in the next moment, and he has a few options. As Rollo May reminds us, there is a space between stimulus and response (May, 1962). Our ability to choose the response is within that space. Does the experience of freedom have any value for the young man, and what can be learned from it?

Much like the known metaphorical distinction between a right and left brain activity, existential thinking distinguishes between a human consciousness that is focused on the subjective experience from the rational one that organizes and catalogues reality in a logical order. The subjective experience (identified with the right brain activity) constitutes the sum of sensual experience that streams to us at any given moment from all our senses—including emotions and will—before those are processed by some interpreting centers (identified with the left, organizing and rational brain activity).

In fact, the subjective consciousness is our experience of reality before 'the voice in our head' organizes it and explains it to us. To experience this, we invite the readers to notice and pause the 'reading voice' in their head for a moment. This would make them notice that parallel to all the ideas that stream from this book to their minds, there are other sensual stimuli. For example, light and colors filling their consciousness, alongside certain scents, voices, physical sensations, and even certain tastes. This is the subjective experience of reading this book, which is unique for this moment, and is unrelated to the written text. It is the part in which Existential thinking aspires to focus, in order to ponder on what that subjective experience is, and what may be learned from it about human psychology and behavior.

In order to answer this question, we delve into a thinking exercise (taken from Jackson, 1986), called 'Mary's Room'. Think about a researcher named Mary, a bright woman who is also a brain scientist specializing in the neurophysiology of vision. Mary dedicates her life to learning everything about the processing of color and light stimuli in the human brain.

Notwithstanding, Mary suffers from a physiological problem; due to a certain fault or radical allergy, exposure to color stimuli might kill her. Therefore, Mary must live all her life in an achromatic cell, protected from any ray of light. From there she researches the world, when all the equipment in her laboratory is black and white, and everything around her is designed to prevent any color stimuli. In fact, Mary has never seen colors in her life.

And so Mary lives, in a black and white prison cell of sorts, from which she explores the world of colors. She understands, so we assume, all that can be learned about color and the way it is experienced by the human mind and translated through reception and processing centers into behaviors and responses. In fact, Mary learned to think of color as mathematic information which is received by a system that applies a very complex algorithm (the human brain). Therefore, she can predict accurately, in any situation, the output (effect on behavior) of any color stimulus on a given person. Reality is also translated into a set of mathematical equations that predict accurately every vision-related stimulus to a specific response. Reality seems to Mary like one big matrix in which the stimuli of colors on human minds can be perfectly predicted.

And now, we get to the bottom line: what will happen if and when scientists develop an antidote to Mary's condition, and suddenly her oversensitivity to color stimuli disappears and she can be exposed to it directly without danger of death? What will happen when Mary sees for the first time the 'blue in the sky' and the 'red in the flowers'? Will the experience of the colorful world include additional and different knowledge to that she already possesses?

If we presume that Mary would learn something new about the world as a result of the change in her condition, we will inevitably conclude that there is knowledge which is not physical about the world. It is perceived through the senses, and not related to our cognitive knowledge about the world. In other words, the 'blueness' of the sky and the 'redness' of the flowers have a different, non-cognitive quality, which is a subjective experience differing from the knowledge that can be acquired about colors through our organizing consciousness. And this kind of 'phenomenal knowledge' is related to one's senses, emotions, and will, not to one's cognitive and organizational skills.

This kind of knowledge can be defined as 'conscious experience', 'first person perspective', or Qualia (Jackson, 1982), that is, the quality of the sensual experience before it is interpreted and translated into meaning for the experiencing person. All the above-mentioned names relate to the way in which a person 'lives' reality separately from how they think about it, in other words, to the lived experience of reality.

To illustrate the difference between those two kinds of categories of consciousness—the organizing one and the 'lived experience', we shall think about scripture for a moment. Look at the letters in the book. Each letter indicates a certain meaning, and together they join into words, sentences, and ideas. The words negotiate ideas to you, the readers, based on the fact that people share common understanding regarding the meaning of the letters and what they symbolize. Now let's assume for a moment that we could somehow stop the work of the rational consciousness, and the letters would lose the meaning that they currently have. Suddenly the letters would seem to you as mysterious runes. You might be able to guess that they signify a meaning, but that meaning itself would no longer be within reach (see Fig. 2.1).

When we look at the old runes without having the key to decipher their meaning, we encounter the subjective experience of consciousness; we experience something, but we cannot interpret it in a distinctive and clear way. The runes may invoke some feelings in us, pictures, scents or other stimuli, perhaps even emotions and will, but we will not be able to understand or construe the meaning without an organizing roadmap of interpretation. In other words, the old runes deliver us a sensual and perhaps emotional experience, without an organizing interpretation. Normally, the lived experience of reality will be brief, because individuals feel awkward in face of reality without having an 'organizing roadmap', so they immediately choose an explanation that is acceptable to them.

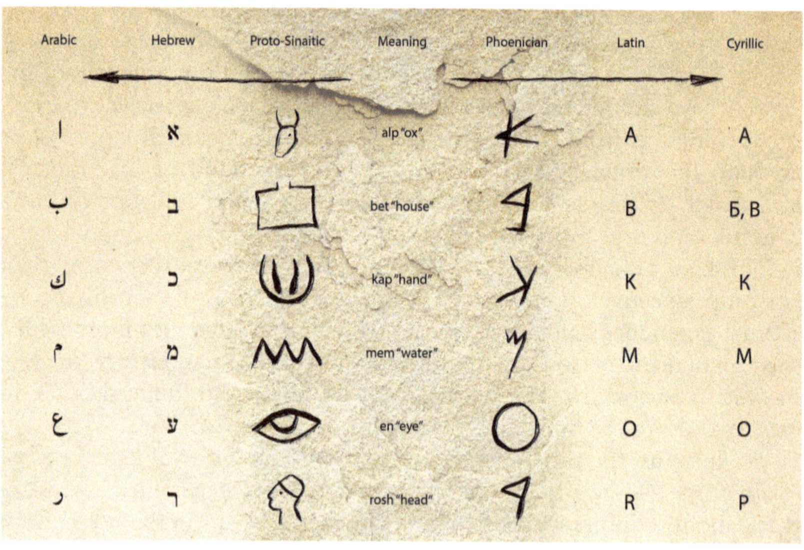

Fig. 2.1 Modern letters and old runes

However, sometimes we can feel the conflict between the two types of consciousness for a longer time, which allows us a glimpse into the depth of the subjective consciousness. An example for this would be transformative life events or experiences, which are powerful occurrences during which people sometimes radically change the way they have been living so far. Looking into such cases should help us understand the pre-interpretational subjective experience.

In order to describe an individual's condition when looking initially at a reality prior to choosing how to interpret it, philosopher Martin Heidegger coined the term 'being here' (Dasein; 1962). It is the primary form of existence of human consciousness before a 'self' or 'personality', which are considered complex terms connected to the interpretive work of the rational mind (the Left brain activity).

Dasein is our consciousness before we choose how to interpret an experience, and how to present it to ourselves, to others and to the world. Dasein is, therefore, an encounter with our potential, a situational freedom that is available for all of us before we decide how to mediate what we feel to ourselves. Dasein is the condition of that French boy before he decided whether to stay home and nurse his mother, or to join the army and fight for the nation—namely, before he decided who he wanted to become. Dasein is the natural condition of every infant in our world who is exposed for the first time to language, sees scriptures, smells and feels various sensations before experience and socialization offer a very specific interpretation to their subjective sensual and emotional experience. The Dasein may also characterize the state of people who have consumed consciousness altering drugs that paralyze the activity of the organizing parts of their mind or in different case people who suffered a medical incident in the brain that influenced its organizing capacity.

Sometimes people encounter their Dasein consciousness spontaneously during forceful events in their lives, when the organizing system is paralyzed because the given person never encountered similar occurrences before, and is lacking a reference point. This may relate to natural disasters and traumatizing events, but also to unexpected happy events and peak experiences. In each of those cases, Dasein constitutes a primary state of consciousness in which an individual goes through an experience, but does not yet possess an interpretation of it. Sometimes such moments are perceived as life changing events, because an individual experiences situational freedom during such moments, where they are not committed to one interpretation of events or another, but are free to choose how to interpret the reality of their life (for more on the relationship between Dasein and life changing events, or transformative life experiences, see Russo-Netzer & Davidov, 2020).

This is also what Sartre (2007) meant when he coined the phrase "existence precedes essence"—that subjective experience of reality precedes the interpreted one. We shall examine such events closely to gain a deep understanding of the Dasein experience. For this purpose, we will first introduce phenomenology which is the theoretical perspective of discussing the lived human experience.

The Existentials of Experience—Hermeneutic Phenomenology

Phenomenology is a general name for a number of different methods and approaches to study the subjective experience. There are two major perspectives of phenomenology in the Western traditional thought, which include the transcendental (or descriptive) and hermeneutic (Kafle, 2011). Descriptive Phenomenology focuses more on a non-interpretive approach to reality and aims to capture subjective experience without using external analysis or interpretation system.

Hermeneutic phenomenology postulates that phenomenological reflection is not introspective but retrospective. In other words, this approach assumes that an experience cannot be comprehended in a pure way, nor understood without some theoretical basis to offer guidelines for interpreting the experience. Hermeneutic phenomenology begins with a descriptive approach to one's subjective experience, followed by a more interpretative one. Interpretation of subjective descriptions tends to rely on the hermeneutic cycle principle, in which the parts of the description can only be understood in the context in which they were accounted for (Kafle, 2011).

Specifically, for the purpose of this book we utilized van Manen's (2016) hermeneutical approach to subjective experience. It postulates that any given subjective experience is always accounted for in the context of the four lifeworld existential modes (also known simply as the 'four existentials'): lived time, lived space, lived body, and lived human relations.

It is important to note that all those terms address a subjective experience, so time is not qualified in minutes; space is not measured in volume or territory units, and so on. Therefore, existential modes of experience refer to felt experience and they are customarily marked by terms like Temporality, Embodiment, Relationality, and Spatiality.

We shall look closely into each of these existential modes of experience, while attempting to distinguish between how they are experienced in normative conditions as opposed to the way they are experienced in life changing events when Dasein prevails.

Temporality

At the heart of every subjective human experience there is, necessarily, a sense of the flowing and rhythm of time. Lived time (i.e. temporality) is an essential domain of experience in which individuals construct their experience to describe who they are in the present in relation to their past experiences and future projections (see Chapman, 1997). Lived time is considered to be contextual (van Manen, 2016), as it plays a part in integrating one's life story into a whole. It may range from past-oriented, slow rhythm or stagnated experience (e.g. living or being occupied with past events, or being a 'thinker') to future-oriented fast rhythm way of life, being a 'doer' (e.g. doing something while thinking of the next thing on the list).

Try recalling a very boring event you have attended recently (a lecture, a work meeting, a long wait for a flight at an airport). Remember the flowing of time during that experience. In this context, it might feel as if time is standing still. A minute may seem like an hour, and even more; an hour at a boring event can be experienced as an eternity (in other words, an 'elongating time' experience), and make the person experiencing it feel exhausted by its end. In contrast, if the event is interesting and engaging, time flies by, and suddenly an hour that goes by seems like five minutes. Sometimes this kind of experience may even induce a sense of freshness and rejuvenation—as opposed to boredom, which makes time stand still. On other occasions it can actually be great stress, such as at the time of an examination, that creates a feeling that time is 'running short', and there is not enough of it.

The flowing of time is also related to different periods and mental states in an individual's life. For example, research on Time Perspective (TP) examined the ways in which the cognitive representation of time changes along different age groups (Baikeli et al., 2021). It found that young people tend to live their lives with a strong emphasis on future orientation, while elderly people tend to live with a stronger emphasis on past orientation. In that way, children experience time as fast-going as compared to adults. For such young children, every moment is full of discovery, curiosity, and fast-paced events. Therefore, they experience every minute as if it was an hour or more in 'adults time'. This is why an evening chat with a toddler, or a child under 10, about what happened in school or kindergarten that same day, is like asking them to remember what happened a month ago. For adults, things are different; time flows in a slow rhythm for them. For an old man 'a year ago' might sometime be experienced as if it was yesterday, because almost no 'felt' time was experienced, as if time never moved.

Similarly, in states of depression, there is often a feeling that time is standing still, or 'stuck'. But during anxiety or general experience of stress, there is a sense of fast and incontrollable flowing of time, like on a roller-coaster, or when time is 'running out'. Thus, in different situations, different life periods and in different contexts—the subjective experience of time is different.

When there is a radical bias toward past orientation, an individual may feel that time slows down, or maybe even pauses, as in 'all will be as it used to be'. Normally, it is accompanied by an experience of boredom and a sense of immobility and rigidity. Individuals in this state may feel that 'there's time', that the pace is slow, and they would tend to be thinkers, namely ponder extensively over their state and the reality of their life.

On the other hand, where there is a strong orientation toward the future (always living in the next moment, a feeling that everything is temporary, an experience of constant change), the flow of time would probably be fast, may cause instability, a sense of chaos, and even anxiety. Generally, the individual in question would be a 'doer', who constantly experiences that 'there is no time', hurries to the next moment in life, lives in a fast pace and prefers constant action.

Most often people feel within the non-extreme ends of the experience, on the range between the next moment (future orientation) and the previous one (past orientation), in an ever-moving pendulum.

A moment for thought: the experience of temporality

- Think about different important social contexts in your life (work, home, extended family etc.), and of your temporal experience in each of them. How does time flow? At work, do you feel that time passes by in a fast or slow pace? And how does it feel at home? How is this experience different when you are alone or when together with other family members? Spouse?

In contrast to the normative experience of temporality that ranges between slow rhythm/past-oriented experience to fast rhythm/future oriented one, the Dasein experience of Temporality is concentrated on the present, the 'now'. The individual is completely focused on the task at hand, the sense of time is pushed aside, and there is a unity of thought and action. Here is an example of such a moment that is all about being in the present, taken from research on transformative life experiences (Russo-Netzer & Davidov, 2020); a moment that has turned into a life-changing experience. This is an excerpt from an in-depth interview with a young Israeli woman, who finished her compulsory military service in Israel and traveled with friends, a short time before she was to embark on an academic studies in order to gain a profession for life. She reported that prior to the event, her life ran its course along a clear program she had in mind of what her life should look like: school, military service, a temporary post-army job, traveling with friends, studying for a profession, embarking on the job market, starting a family, and so on. She was at the stage of "travelling with friends", just before starting her planned Business Management studies, when a transformative life experience took place. This event that took place in Rhodes while sitting in an old city café changed her life's course in a profound way, so that, instead of proceeding to business school, she decided to learn psychology and therapy. Here is an excerpt from her interview:

> *When I was 21 I went to Greece with friends who I'm no longer in touch with now, as in, friends I had around my work or job, people I knew who went to Greece. People I knew looked for someone to go with them. It was an opportunity for me. We had an amazing trip. I, together with one guy, sort of broke away from the group ... and we wandered about, we were in Rhodes, we rolled into this alleyway, it was quiet, quiet, quiet. Suddenly there was a sign in English that there is, like, a café on the roof. And we went up there and everything there was white and we were the only ones there ... I remember the ... it wasn't sofas it was like wooden chairs, and everything was so white ... And I only remember that the only noise we heard was a hammer hitting on a nail. And it was absolutely quiet there. We sat quietly both of us. I am a person of many words. Suddenly I became peaceful and also sad. I told my friend that I am experiencing the feeling I never felt before, that I am doing nothing, that the moment has no meaning, and that I am just BEING, as in, I realized this moment had never happened to me before. And I think from that moment on something awakened in me and was actively seeking this serenity.*

In this description, we can see how the interviewee experiences one "moment" that changes her life, when she experiences a "quiet" moment that "meant nothing". When we try to understand what is so special about that moment in the context of her account, it is discernible that normally the interviewee experiences the flowing of time as something that is always fast paced and oriented toward the future; toward the next moment in her life—from work to travel to university, to something else she refers to as "life" and "everything". Suddenly, this experience is disrupted by one contextless moment, in the sense that it is not just another moment in a sequence of moments, it is not connected to and it does not precede another moment; it is a "moment in its own rights", which has a "brightness of light" and a lot of quietness. It is a constituting moment, which the young woman keeps searching for in her life over and over again.

In our terms, the interviewee indicates that the flow of time had changed, and instead of being oriented toward some future (university, job, life, etc.), she became tuned to the present moment, which drew her attention. In other words, from a situation where time flows in fast rhythm, it slowed does significantly here, and all of a sudden, she turned her full attention to the sounds surrounding her, scents, colors. All that exists for one magical moment is that café in Rhodes. Namely, all that exists in the moment of Dasein is the present, the 'now', with no past or future orientation. This break in the normative flow of time that an individual is used to is what enables and opens up the possibility of making a profound change in life.

Similarly, Mihaly Csikszentmihalyi (1990), discovered an experience he named 'Flow', comprised of common characteristics including an experience of presence embedded in the current moment. The state of Flow is an optimal experience of internal motivation, in which the individual is completely absorbed in an activity which becomes its own purpose, rather than aimed at an external reward.

The synergy between thoughts and action, which is typical to the Flow experience, is the main thing differentiating it from other day to day situations in which attention is split. In the Flow experience, the individuals become a part of the activity they engage in, as if the act and the actor become one. Accordingly, the Flow experience is characterized by focus and concentration. During the Flow experience, the future and the past dispel, facing the tangibility of the present; matters unrelated to the activity are pushed away from attention. Therefore, this kind of experience that involves deep focus, full presence and concentration may lead to the experience of being now.

Embodiment

Embodiment is another mode of experience that refers to the phenomenological idea that individuals are always present in the world as a subject (van-Manen, 2016). This term is also known as corporality in parallel phenomenological tradition (e.g. Husserl, 2012). It is an essential domain of experience in which an account represents one's felt body, ranging from comfortable freedom and high-impact presence to limited, low-impact presence. This experience is not necessarily associated with actual physical size, as for example a person who is considered over-weight in terms of height-weight ratio (BMI), may feel themself to be undersized and belittled when facing frightening experience such as under assault of other people.

The experience of embodiment is dynamic and ever-changing throughout the hours of the day and life periods. It remains so through various developmental stages like puberty and old age, or various social contexts. For instance, a person appearing on stage and receiving cheers and applauds from an audience may feel their presence extends to be larger and wider—namely, a sense of empowerment and grandeur of a high impact presence. In contrast, an individual who experienced themselves as facing danger and threat might experience low-impact presence that might include self-restraint, undersized, inferiority, and meekness.

The embodiment experience is apparent, for example, in authority-relationships; an employee would normally feel restrained, and prefer to be humble and keep low-impact presence in the company of a higher authority, yet decisive and prominent high impact presence in face of subordinates. The term 'embodiment' therefore emphasizes the way in which the experience of being present in a given moment materializes. As noted, the experience of embodiment moves on a range between a sense of low-impact and diminished presence on one end, and a high-impact characterized by extended presence, on the other.

A moment for thought: The Embodiment experience

- Think about various meaningful places for you (work, home, being in nature etc.) Consider your physical sensation of presence in each of those places. What do they invoke in you? Low or high impact presence? Restraint or decisiveness? Diminishment or expansion? Gumption or need for support? How do you change in-between the different contexts?

During a Dasein experience of being here and now the embodiment turns into a sense of **presence and flexibility**, which enables the process of becoming as far as self-perception and self-value are concerned. It enables one to simply be in the event, without feeling diminished, empowered, or biased in any other way. Therefore, they are also unpredictable and ever emerging, depending on the context in which they are present.

This sensation arises also from the previous excerpt (the Rhodes account) which emphasized the presence in the moment, and indeed they are intertwined and often inseparable. Yet, some accounts are more focused on the embodiment aspect of the here and now Dasein experience. It is a non-judgmental presence in the moment; and it is accounted from a somewhat distant vantage point.

The following excerpt demonstrates the above. During meditation, the interviewee suddenly experiences a transformative life experience, described through a corporal-embodiment account. The following event exhibits an experience that led to an essential change in the interviewee's professional life—from a natural science scholar to an interest in humanities, specifically engaged in studying the holocaust and the history of the Jewish people. It is apparent that the experience itself enables her to be present, and therefore be flexible about her self-perception:

> *I felt like my physical body can't contain what was going on inside me, it's like I had some kind of an expansion inside … I don't know how to define it, I felt it in my heart. Like my heart opens up more and more until my body cannot contain it and it is about to crush to pieces and I didn't know what to do with it … And it did something in my heart, this openness, it is hard to express in words … it is very destabilizing experience, but also profoundly crystalizing. You slowly see things so clearly, it's an experience that changes everything I was raised on all my life. You become different afterwards. This experience really opened a crack in my square and closed world … I came back a different person, I could see that what happened to me does not define my identity; it is I who decide who I am going to be.*

In descriptions demonstrating the Dasein experience through embodiment we often see the change described through the prism of what happens to the self-perception of the interviewee. Interviewees describe it as a moment in which their perception of themselves suddenly changes. In that moment, they find themselves present, as they are, without any thoughts about who they are supposed to be. This observation of themselves without filters or judgment may constitute a thorough change in their life, because it enables flexibility in all that concerns identity and self-worth.

In the description of the experience here, the interviewee practiced meditation and suddenly found herself present in the moment, looking at her own body and the processes that took place in it, without applying judgment or thought. Out of the changes of the body, her own self-perception changes; namely, from the experience of being present grows a different perception of the self, which changes the interviewee's life. This is a challenging presence, which re-examines what the individual takes for granted. And again, at the heart of the Dasein experience, the split between the corporal experience and the individual's judgment of what one should be is momentarily canceled, and briefly a pure experience of embodiment emerges; a challenging presence that enables an individual to experience themself as an ever emerging process rather than a fixed entity.

Relationality

Lived human relations (relationality) refer to the idea that individuals are always immersed in relationships with others (van Manen, 2016). It is an essential domain of experience ranging from complete fusion with others (i.e. being a team player) to separation and a deep sense of isolation (i.e. lone wolf type). Along these lines, van Manen (2016) asserts that for example the lived experience of a teacher must involve a relationship with his\her students, much like the lived experience of a parent which inevitably involves a relationship with a child, or the lived experience of a pastor which involves reference to his\her community.

Relationality plays an essential role in the social construction of identity and the subjective experience of reality, as suggested in various fields, such as social construction (Gergen, 1991), social identity theory (Tajfel & Turner, 1979), attachment theory (Bowlby, 1969). The centrality of rationality has been demonstrated in many studies, such as the social construction of race (Smedley & Smedley, 2005); of technology (Klein & Kleinman, 2002); of illness (Conrad & Barker, 2010); or the social construction of gender, all of which are constructed along performance in a range of settings and activities and in relation to other people (Courtenay, 2000). In the era of social networks, this issue of social comparing and our self-perception in relation to others is more poignant than ever. Constant exposure in social networks to filtered and unrealistic images of success, happiness and achievement may impact individuals' self-perceptions—from a person in their own rights, into a product in the global market.

In this context, individuals might feel invisible, inconsequent, or devoid of value. One of the expressions of the awkwardness, stress, and anxiety involved in social comparisons is embedded in the notion of FOMO (Fear of Missing Out). This phenomenon is amplified especially in the social networks, where we are exposed to satisfying experiences of others, that underline our own sense of missing out—which might lead to paralysis, avoidance, and stagnation. It has been discovered, for example, that FOMO is connected to behavioral, emotional and motivational aspects of social anxiety (see Przybylski et al., 2013). To summarize, the relational experience ranges between isolation to fusion. On the one hand, we find isolation incompatibility, loneliness, and the need to be different and unique, as illustrated in the 'my interest comes first' or a 'lone wolf' stance toward others. On the other hand, we find fusion and lack of distinctiveness as illustrated in the 'to be considerate of others' or a 'team player' position toward others.

A moment for thought: The Relationality experience

- Think again about significant places for you (work, home, nature, gym, coffee-shop etc.), and about your own experience vis-à-vis the other actors in those spaces. Now, focus on the significant others who populate the different spaces in your life. What connections do you have with significant others in your life? do you tend to be 'team players' or 'lone wolves'? Do you prefer to emphasize the ways in which you are different? Or do you hide it and bring out the mutual and similar?

Compared to the relatively prevailing range, the Dasein experience cancels, momentarily, the relationality, and emphasizes a sense of unity, fraternity, and belonging with significant others, while maintaining singularity and not getting absorbed into the crowd; or, in other words, 'being together' with others while maintaining unique individuality.

The following excerpts demonstrate this sense of unity and lack of relationality, both toward humans and objects. The first is from a girl who lived a raucous life: after being abused at home she deteriorated to living at the edge of delinquency, and was moved from one institute to the next, getting into trouble every single time. Generally, until the event described in the excerpt had taken place, the girl experienced herself as a marginal and insignificant character in the society in which she lived. But then comes that moment, in the boarding school she stayed in while in the ninth grade (age 15); a moment after which she opens up to society and becomes a part of her own community:

> *Towards the end of the school year of 9th grade there was a night when me and all the others from my year sat together and just talked. We opened our hearts to each other and established some closeness and understanding. It was like a feeling that I was being accepted as I am, no matter what I went through and how many things about me were bad; Just acceptance, no matter what. It was an event that made me realize that I found my place, I found amazing friends, friends who can understand me with an open and flowing discourse. Other than this social aspect, the boarding school and the staff were amazing, and yes that was the moment when the penny dropped, and I found my safe and serene place, and ever since then the boarding school became a home for me; just like that. Because as far as I was concerned, I never really had a home, and in the boarding school I did find it.*

In the Dasein experience, there is a moment in which relationality to others is canceled, and the individual feels as if there is no screen or barrier between them and significant others. A sense of partnership and connection emerges, as if the other is another version of the experiencing individual. There is no need to hide anything from them or hide from them—because that would be like hiding from oneself.

In the description, the interviewee experiences for the first time an 'opening of the heart' to others. She suddenly discovers that there is no need any more to conceal 'the bad', because she is a part of the others and they are a part of her. The individual as a whole feels one with their environment; therefore, it is an experience of unity and belonging to a certain group or culture, from a position that maintains the uniqueness and singularity of the experiencing person. This sense of unity that is typical to Dasein is aimed at the whole environment, and sometimes even at inhuman objects, like in the following case:

> *We camped outdoors in nature and I got up early in the morning because I used to get up early and meditate, and this time I was in nature and it was ... there was some stream there, and I sat on a rock listening to the stream and felt the*

water actually flow through me, and suddenly that connection of the ... silence with the water, it is very—very strong, I actually reached peace I am like the water, so the water flow through me and I felt like I was water myself, so it was a few minutes of grace, that I received. Everything was breathing, I saw the trees live, I saw everything breath, I can't explain it, it's hard ... It was not an experience I can really describe in words too much, it ...

In this excerpt, the unity is with objects in nature, the water flow, and the trees, and for a moment, the experience of relativity and distance between the individual and the outside world is eliminated. A sense of harmony and balance is established between 'self' and 'others'. In other words, in a moment of Dasein, an individual experiences external objects and people as if they are connected and harmonious. This harmony, this sense of 'togetherness' is what frees an individual for a moment from the relations which bind them until that moment. It enables situational freedom and the possibility of generating a significant change in the way a person experiences their life's reality.

Spatiality

At the heart of every experience, there is an element of space, as it is perceived subjectively—namely, Spatiality. It is an essential domain of experience in which individuals construct an account as to what is in the foreground and what is in the background, reflecting what is considered meaningful and marginal to them (see Valle & King, 1978). In essence, the experience of felt space encompasses both physical and social boundaries. As such, it ranges from closed, secured, inflexible boundaries, including strict social regularities, to borderless boundaries and alienated, chaotic social order.

An experience cannot take place without spatiality. Have a look, for example, at the place in which you are reading this book—be it your room, the local café, a beach, or an airport. Observe the space for a minute. Every space where you are present is necessarily 'yours', in the sense that your experience is unique. Another person, even a friend or a family member, would essentially experience it somewhat differently.

For example, if two people walk together on a beach—the beach would seem a bit different for each of them. Each would describe it in slightly different words and notice different details in the situation. Consequently, the space would turn into a different place in their experience. Thus, if one of them were interested in water sports, for instance, they'd notice the state of the water, the height of the waves, speed of the wind, and so on. At the same time, the other, who is a culinary buff, might check out the restaurants and try to figure out the menus, or think of a meal to match the atmosphere. A third person might surf on the wings of imagination and follow the feelings invoked in them by the seaside, and so on. All this happens because our experience of space is subjective. Therefore, the significant thing for an individual about a certain place would be, for them, in the foreground of the experience. What is less important for the individual remains in the background (see the gestalt principles of perception, for example, in Koffka, 2013).

Generally, there are people who prefer the presence of a space that is familiar and stable—'a clear and set space' with known rules, regulations, and order. Others thrive in a space where unpredictability, alienation and even danger, or chaos of 'no clear borders', prevail. That is to say, the main characteristic is the sense of boundaries which a space bestows upon us, ranging between a clear and enclosed space (including law and order) to an open ended one (all the way to chaotic).

To exemplify this last point, research has found that people tend to better recover from medical conditions in their own familiar domestic environment, compared to people in hospital settings, where space is often experienced as alienated (Tembo, 2016). Such discoveries have led modern medicine to consider more outsourcing of the healing process to the homes of the clients, rather than concentrate them in one place (the hospital) that projects alienation and damages their healing prospects. The design of a physical environment has emotional, cognitive, and social impact on individuals.

Another example is taken from workspaces and their influence on the quality of individuals' work. Whether we work in an office building, a factory, a warehouse, a café or at home, in an open space or in meeting rooms, we function in a physical space. The features of the physical space are intertwined with psychological characteristics such as status, privacy, ownership, and control. Research has shown that the physical environment in which humans live and operate has a significant influence over their feeling and ability to function (Colenberg et al., 2020). One of the expressions of its far-reaching influence is a phenomenon known as 'the sick building syndrome' (Ghaffarianhoseini et al., 2018). In the modern work environment, this syndrome often effects offices devoid of sun light, with internal air conditioning, fluorescent lightning, and lack of movement. Studies found a connection between those features and employees' complaints about difficulties to concentrate, fatigue, and even absences from work and physical illness.

Exposing the syndrome has led to growing awareness to the importance of physical working environments that takes into account elements of 'green construction'. A connection was established between 'green construction' and improvement in employees' and school pupils' satisfaction and functioning. Those examples demonstrate the psychological, physical, and cognitive influence of the physical environment.

In summary, spatiality ranges from the structured 'there is a space' experience, with clear rules, boundaries, and regulations, to the chaotic 'no space' experience, with its chaotic, flexible, and free space.

But in addition, there is also the **Dasein** experience of spatiality, when the individuals experience themselves as being here in a holistic way. For one moment, the whole organization of reality according to what is more important (Fig. 2.1) and what is less so (background)—is eliminated. The space becomes enabling and supportive of change, it is dynamic and malleable to 'play' with, namely, given to influence by the individual present in it. This experience of space enables establishing a significant change in the way people understand their lives, and reorganize what is significant in them.

The following excerpt demonstrates a 'being-here' Dasein experience. It introduces a transformative life experience told by a 50 year old woman. It describes a moment that took place when she was ten years old, and she was told that her mother is dying of a disease. In that moment, she had decided to change the way she lives, and her priorities.

> *I was at home; it was the summer holiday, so they made sure to put me in all the possible summer day-cares to keep me away, so that I wouldn't feel the hardship, because everybody knew where this was heading. She was nearing the end. On that day I deliberately missed my ride. I stayed at home, and then my father drove with me to the hospital, but they refused to let me in. This I don't remember that well, I remember my sister coming out of my mother's room crying, and then we went downstairs. I don't remember if I went into the room or not, and I remember we sat on the grass, and I can tell you the lawn was not mowed that day, the grass was terribly, terribly, high, and uncomfortable to sit on. And then they told me that my mother died …* it was as if the ground trembled beneath me. *I don't even remember whether I cried or not? Am I allowed to cry? I was quiet. Nobody else spoke. The only thing I remember was the height of the grass. We didn't speak and we didn't cry either.*

In this case, in the moment when the interviewee receives the news of her mother's death, she experienced that 'the ground trembled beneath her. In other words, the moment does not have a defined place in which she is present. Such phrases are typical of this mode of experience, with variations like "the sky fell over my head" or "the carpet was pulled out from under"', etc. What those phrases have in common is the attempt to capture the experience where there is no distinct and obvious space with a clear figure and a defined background.

In other words, there is no prioritizing of what is central and what is marginal in the experience. Thus, the interviewee does not know how to behave, because there is no organizing system for the subjective experience. She doesn't know whether to cry or not, what to think or what to do. All that exists is what's in front of her—the lawn where she was sitting on upon receiving the news.

Therefore, unlike a normative spatial experience that is organized between the important and the less important, the unbalanced and the stable, the true and the unreal—the Dasein experience allows the individual to be present in a space without arranging it according to some internal order which gives every element in the experience a clear meaning.

This breaking of the normative organizational system enables individuals to generate a profound change in their life, and grants them situational freedom to experience their reality differently. The lived space is experienced through the senses and not through rational thinking, which breaks down familiar patterns and allow the individual to 'play' with different and fresh new interpretations of his experience. In this case, it enabled the girl to mourn her mother without being confined to existing patterns of "the right thing to do" in such a situation.

Finally, we can say that the day-to-day lifeworld experience of individuals ranges between fast pace (getting ready for the next moment) and slow rhythm (reflecting over previous moments) of life (temporality); between a low and high impact sense of self (embodiment); between fusion and separation sense of relationship with others (relationality); and between clear and blurry boundaries (spatiality). Felt experience is like a hurricane; consciousness sways from one feeling to another according to the context we experience. It shifts from slow to fast rhythm, low to high impact presence, isolation to fusion and so on. In this state, there is no situational freedom because the split consciousness always applies a certain interpretation of reality according to pre-defined organizing system. Thus, we are confined to a certain script or world-view, which can be also seen as 'core beliefs', that largely determine our lived experience in any given context.

Yet, just like a hurricane, the storm has a center of gravitas, or 'the eye of the storm'. There, everything calms down, the emotional movements stop, and the split consciousness turns into one, focused in the moment, in the here and now. This is the Dasein experience, which includes presence in the time and the place, flexibility in self-perception and a sense of 'being together' with others. This is also the experience that enables situational freedom, because in such moments individuals can choose how to interpret their reality and what is meaningful for them in a specific context (prioritizing meaning, see Russo-Netzer, 2018). They can influence and change it according to their intentions and will; be a part of reality rather than a passive participant.

The connection between the Dasein experience and the ability to change is demonstrated in many studies examining the individual's experience in the context of turning points and life changing events. Those are cases where a certain human way of living goes through a significant change during a certain event, and is replaced by a different way. Such turning points take place during mental trauma (Calhoun & Tedeschi, 2006; Linley & Joseph, 2004), when mourning a significant other (Polatinsky & Esprey, 2000), during serious or terminal illness (Hefferon et al., 2009), and sometimes during terror attacks or radically violent events (Williams, 2007).

Turning points characterize life events that undermine existing core beliefs and meaning systems which individuals hold regarding the realities of their life. They facilitate the conditions that enable individuals to observe the organizing basic assumptions of their life, and a willingness to change them (Janoff-Bulman, 1992; Park, 2010; Park & Folkman, 1997).

Furthermore, recent studies about transformative life experiences showed that the experience of change is highly related to being present in the here and now. This condition facilitates openness to various new possibilities of choice, and ways of being in the world that the individual was not previously aware of (Russo-Netzer & Davidov, 2020). Based on that study and others, we can argue that any significant change of an individual involves such an encounter with the Dasein experience of here-and-now. In other worlds, the Dasein is the experience of the space that lies between stimulus and response, that enables situational freedom, choice and subsequently change, growth, and development.

The following chart (Table 2.1) summarizes what was presented so far.

Table 2.1 The subjective conscious experience map

Existential Mode of experience	*Split consciousness, focused on 'there is not' experience*	*Dasein, being here, un-interpreted experience*	*Split consciousness, focused on 'what exists/ there is' experience*
Temporality	A 'there is no time' experience, future orientation. 'Being in action', the individual lives in a fast pace	**Being now**, merging thought and action (flow)	A 'there is time' experience, past orientation, 'pondering', the individual lives in slow pace
Embodiment	A 'no self' experience, low-impact presence	**Being present,** flexibility and changing, unpredictability, forming	An experience of 'existing self', high-impact presence,
Relationality	A 'no others' experience, isolation, lone wolf, A need to be different	**Being together** Partnership between equals	A 'there are others' experience, fusion, team player, being 'like everybody else'
Spatiality	A 'no space—Open space' experience A need for open chaotic space with no clear rules	**Being here** A dynamic feeling, ability to influence the space in both physical and social aspects	A 'there is a structured space' experience The need for clear law and order

Here arises the question—what stops us from staying in the Dasein experience in the long run? Why can't most of us experience it without using special means such as meditation or consciousness-changing drugs, or during transformative life experiences? In other words, why can't we experience 'being here' also while speaking to our spouses or colleagues? Or when we are in the endless daily race of life, managing the tasks we must complete within a given time? We shall offer here an answer derived from the depth of existential thought and related to the Dasein experience and the freedom it can enable. As previously explained (see Chap. 1), the experience of freedom is related to the anxiety of guilt and to a responsibility that is hard to bear. In the next chapter we will demonstrate that the here-and-now Dasein experience is a necessary but not sufficient condition for facilitating change. This is due to it lacking the element of constant awareness of the individual's perpetual changing process. In the next chapter we examine this "awareness of changing" (i.e. authenticity), which is the other distinctive element of the Dasein experience.

References

Baikeli, R., Li, D., Zhu, L., & Wang, Z. (2021). The relationship between time perspective and meaning in life across different age stages in adulthood. *Personality and Individual Differences, 174*. https://doi.org/10.1016/j.paid.2021.110668

Bowlby, J. (1969). *Attachment and loss, vol. I: Attachment*. Basic Books.

Calhoun, L. G., & Tedeschi, R. G. (2006). The foundations of posttraumatic growth: An expanded framework. In L. G. Calhoun & R. G. Tedeschi (Eds.), *The handbook of posttraumatic growth: Research and practice* (pp. 1–23). Erlbaum.

Chapman, M. D. (1997). Time in human life. In H. R. Pollio, T. B. Henley, & C. J. Thompson (Eds.), *The phenomenology of everyday life* (pp. 93–123). Cambridge University Press. https://doi.org/10.1017/CBO9780511752919

Colenberg, S., Jylhä, T., & Arkesteijn, M. (2020). The relationship between interior office space and employee health and well-being—A literature review. *Building Research & Information, 49*(3), 352. https://doi.org/10.1080/09613218.2019.1710098

Conrad, P., & Barker, K. K. (2010). The social construction of illness: Key insights and policy implications. *Journal of Health and Social Behavior, 51*(Suppl. 1), S67–S79. https://doi.org/10.1177/0022146510383495

Courtenay, W. H. (2000). Constructions of masculinity and their influence on men's well-being: A theory of gender and health. *Social Science & Medicine, 50*(10), 1385–1401. https://doi.org/10.1016/S0277-9536(99)00390-1

Csikszentmihalyi, M. (1990). *Flow: The psychology of optimal experience*. Harper & Row.

Gergen, K. J. (1991). *The saturated self: Dilemmas of identity in contemporary life* (Vol. 166). Basic books.

Ghaffarianhoseini, A., AlWaer, H., Omrany, H., Ghaffarianhoseini, A., Alalouch, C., Clements-Croome, D., & Tookey, J. (2018). Sick building syndrome: Are we doing enough? *Architectural Science Review, 61*(3), 99–121.

Hefferon, K., Grealy, M., & Mutrie, N. (2009). Post-traumatic growth and life-threatening physical illness: A systematic review of the qualitative literature. *British Journal of Health Psychology, 14*(2), 343–378.

Heidegger, M. (1962). *Being and time* (J. Macquarrie & E. Robinson, Trans.). Blackwell.

Husserl, E. (2012). *Ideas: General introduction to pure phenomenology*. Routledge.

Jackson, F. (1982). Epiphenomenal qualia. *The Philosophical Quarterly, 32*(127), 127–136.

Jackson, F. (1986). What Mary didn't know. *The Journal of Philosophy, 83*(5), 291–295.

Janoff-Bulman, R. (1992). *Shattered assumptions: Towards a new psychology of trauma*. Free Press.

Kafle, N. P. (2011). Hermeneutic phenomenological research method simplified. *Bodhi: An Interdisciplinary Journal, 5*(1), 181–200. https://doi.org/10.3126/bodhi.v5i1.8053

Klein, H. K., & Kleinman, D. L. (2002). The social construction of technology: Structural considerations. *Science, Technology, & Human Values, 27*(1), 28–52. https://doi.org/10.1177/016224390202700102

Koffka, K. (2013). *Principles of gestalt psychology*. Routledge.

Linley, P. A., & Joseph, S. (2004). Positive change following trauma and adversity: A review. *Journal of Traumatic Stress, 17*(1), 11–21. https://doi.org/10.1023/B:JOTS.0000014671.27856.7e

May, R. (1962). Freedom and responsibility re-examined. In *Unpublished paper read at the 1962 meeting of the American College Personnel Association* (pp. 44–52). Chicago.

Park, C. L. (2010). Making sense of the meaning literature: An integrative review of meaning making and its effects on adjustment to stressful life events. *Psychological bulletin, 136*(2), 257.

Park, C. L., & Folkman, S. (1997). Meaning in the context of stress and coping. *Review of General Psychology, 1*(2), 115–144.

Polatinsky, S., & Esprey, Y. (2000). An assessment of gender differences in the perception of benefit resulting from the loss of a child. *Journal of Traumatic Stress, 13*(4), 709–718. https://doi.org/10.1023/A:1007870419116

Przybylski, A. K., Murayama, K., DeHaan, C. R., & Gladwell, V. (2013). Motivational, emotional, and behavioral correlates of fear of missing out. *Computers in Human Behavior, 29*(4), 1841–1848.

Russo-Netzer, P. (2018). Prioritizing meaning as a pathway to meaning in life and general well-being. *Journal of Happiness Studies, 20*(6), 1863–1891. https://doi.org/10.1007/s10902-018-0031-y

Russo-Netzer, P., & Davidov, J. (2020). Transformative life experience as a glimpse into potentiality. *Journal of Humanistic Psychology, 0022167820937487.*

Sartre, J. P. (2007). *Existentialism is a humanism* (C. Macomber, Trans.). Yale University Press.

Smedley, A., & Smedley, B. D. (2005). Race as biology is fiction, racism as a social problem is real: Anthropological and historical perspectives on the social construction of race. *American Psychologist, 60*(1), 16–26. https://doi.org/10.1037/0003-066X.60.1.16

Tajfel, H., & Turner, J. C. (1979). An integrative theory of intergroup conflict. In W. G. Austin & S. Worchel (Eds.), *The social psychology of intergroup relations* (pp. 33–47). Brooks/Cole.

Tembo, A. C. (2016). Phenomenological inquiry as a methodology for investigating the lived experience of being critically ill in intensive care. *Journal of Intensive and Critical Care, 2*(1), 17.

Valle, R. S., & King, M. (1978). *Existential-phenomenological alternatives for psychology*. Oxford University Press.
Van Manen, M. (2016). Researching lived experience: Human science for an action sensitive pedagogy. *Routledge*.
Williams, R. (2007). The psychosocial consequences for children of mass violence, terrorism and disasters. *International Review of Psychiatry, 19*(3), 263–277. https://doi.org/10.1080/09540260701349480

CHAPTER 3

Authenticity and the Four Universal Concerns

Abstract This chapter explores the essence of subjective experience, and particularly how it is influenced by existential anxiety, which is typically defined as becoming aware of the universal concerns of human existence, including the concepts of death, freedom, isolation, and meaninglessness. According to existential thought, such awareness to our existential concerns often provokes negative emotions such as fear and dread, and is considered to be the bedrock of all everyday worries and fears in human life. Most people can deploy defense mechanisms to cope with this anxiety, but the distraction and evasion mechanisms they deploy to shift attention from the universal concerns, in order to gain a sense of safety and security, are considered an inauthentic way of being in the world that might be the cause of psychopathology. Based on existing literature, we delineate a possible conceptual roadmap to illustrate that inauthenticity and authenticity are not separate modes but rather reflect a range of possible responses to the universal concerns across a wide spectrum. Authenticity is introduced as a balanced approach to one's existential anxiety and thus a central aspect of the intervention process.

Keywords Heidegger • Situational freedom • Nothingness • Groundlessness • The absurd • Existential anxiety • The universal concern of Death • The universal concern of Freedom • The universal concern of Isolation • The universal concern of Meaninglessness • Authenticity

J. Davidov, P. Russo-Netzer, *Existential Authenticity*,
https://doi.org/10.1007/978-3-031-07842-2_3

Heidegger (1962) was the first to distinguish between two levels of consciousness. The first is a level that acknowledges freedom embedded in the Dasein experience, also known as 'the authentic existence'. The second level suppress the idea of freedom and prefers a forgetfulness-of-being state of mind, also known as the 'inauthentic existence'.

The first level of consciousness refers to being mindful of our existence. It implies accepting the experience of freedom and being aware of the fact that the experiences of nothingness and groundlessness precede our interpretation of them. In other words—our existence precedes our essence (e.g. Sartre, 2007). Heidegger called this state an 'authentic state of existence' (Heidegger, 1962), and noted that while in it we are aware that who we have become (our 'essence') is a result of our choices. Thus, we are aware that we are free and responsible for the reality we experience. We are aware of ourselves as beings that constantly organize, construct, and find meaning in our reality in a subjective way.

In other words, as authentic beings, we realize that in each and every moment we choose how to react and conduct ourselves. Thus, we are full participants in fulfilling a certain reality over another, and in **creating a different reality** to the one we had a moment ago. In what we say or do not say, in what we choose to do and not—we partake in what we shall experience in our reality, and what we will miss out on.

The experience of existential freedom, therefore, is based on two elements—the choice (intertwined with the Dasein experience), and the awareness of the constant changing nature of the perceived experience—which is the authentic existence. An individual may encounter the Dasein experience while meditating or exercising, or even spontaneously while traveling. This experience, in turn, may expose them to different ways of living. As noted, this experience is a necessary condition for freedom because it enhances the element of choice in life. It may influence decisions that a person may take regarding their life and how they want to live it. However, it is not a satisfactory condition for freedom, because it does not emphasize the experience of change itself. Change involves the constant shift in the way reality is perceived and experienced.

This can be demonstrated by a story about an old wise man in a small village in the mountains. The man was famous for his wisdom and as one who has an answer for any query and question. In that same village lived a mischievous child, who decided to test the old man's wisdom. He caught a butterfly, and hid it in the palm of his hand. He said to himself "I'll ask the old man what is in my fist. I suppose he is wise enough to know that it is a butterfly, and he will say so. Then, I'll ask another question, a trick question: is it alive or dead? If the man says 'alive', I'll squeeze the butterfly in my hand until it dies; and if he will say 'dead', I'll open my palm, set the butterfly free—and prove him wrong".

The child went over to the old man to pull his trick. When the boy faced the old man and asked what is in his hand, the man replied, "that's a butterfly". And then, the child asked the trick-question: "Is it alive or dead?". The old man gave him a long stare and replied, "this is in your hand".

The story demonstrates the element of choice. The child, like all of us, is the one who decides in each moment what will happen in the next—what will and will not be said, what will live and what will die. This is true for every instance in our life: What shall we say in the next moment to our spouse? Our boss? Our children? Our parents? How shall we behave? In every moment, there is situational freedom to choose between a few alternatives for managing ourselves in the next moment, and this determines the course of our life. In every moment we experience our Dasein, situational freedom, and through such freedom of choice we take part in the creation of our experience.

Let's examine a day-to-day situation in which two people find themselves in similar circumstances which may yield two possible modes of action. In other words—they can decide whether to kill the butterfly, or let it live. Both of them experience Dasein for a brief segment, as they take a decision: how should they behave? What will their experience in the next moment? One possibility would be to make a choice and then justify it to afterwards. Such position would be a deterministic one, suggesting that "I do not have a choice because this is who I am and there is no other option given these circumstances".

Another possibility, the authentic one, would maintain the awareness that there several alternatives exist. This entails an acknowledgement of the possible doubts and the existential uncertainty involved with making a choice. Killing the butterfly or letting it go—are both irrevocable actions. Both options determine the way reality may change accordingly.

The path of the authentic person is similar to walking on the brink of an abyss, where a bridge is only created when we dare to stretch a foot forward and place it on the void in front of us. In every moment, we are aware that how we behave, what we say, do, or refrain from doing—changes our life experience. It essentially implies that the current moment is unique, unrepeatable and will never return in the same way.

The authentic state of consciousness involves a direct encounter with an experience of groundlessness and nothingness, which lies in the essence of making a choice (Heidegger, 1962).

At this point, it is important to distinguish between two close concepts that are sometimes used interchangeably: authenticity and genuinity 'authenticity' in. The authenticity we refer to in this book focuses on the awareness of change embedded in our situational freedom. Genuinity, however, focuses on the experience of being true to one's values, in alignment with, thoughts, emotions, and behaviors (Ryan & Ryan, 2019). The concept of genuinity involves the idea of 'true self' which exists at the core of every individual's being (James, 1958; Kierkegaard, 2013; Winnicott, 2018). The more an individual is incongruence with his or her true self, they live in a way that reflects their values and beliefs, rather than following external norms and cultural expectations influenced by the society in general (Fromm, 2000). Numerous studies emphasize the importance of genuinity, oftentimes referred to as authenticity, to individuals' self-perception, self-worth, psychological well-being, and meaning in life (e.g., Ilies et al., 2005; Lakey et al., 2008; Schlegel et al., 2011).

However, it can be suggested that genuinity and its related relationship with the 'true self' concept is a function of the 'left brain' (i.e., organizing and rational) consciousness. It views individuals as entities who regulate their thoughts and behaviors based on a set of given core beliefs and values which consist their 'true self'. Alternatively, living authentically means living in a way that resonates with the subjective, non-rational experience of Dasein, which is a function of the right brain consciousness. This is a significant distinction, which might even be conflicting, as illustrated in the story of Abraham and the binding of Isaac (Kierkegaard, 2013).

The binding of Isaac is a non-rational act which contradicts reasonable moral values, and therefore cannot be explained rationally. This is the state of mind which Abraham must have experienced from the minute he left his tent, traveling to the Moriah Mountain to sacrifice his son and up until new possibilities surfaced—namely the ram that replaced Isaac on the altar at the last moment. Thus, the authentic state of mind is intertwined with an experience of absurdity in which people cannot rationalize their choices to themselves or their environment (Golomb, 2012). The absurd experience can be referred to as the bedrock of existential anxiety surrounding authenticity as it implies the uncertainty and groundlessness of the authentic act.

When people follow the principles of reason and moral, they may experience gratifying achievement and success in a given society. Yet they may still feel an existential vacuum because they do not live their life authentically. At the center of such experience there is an absurd that cannot be rationally explained.

This absurd encapsulates the existential anxiety. We shall, therefore, examine this existential anxiety in detail, and explore its different components.

The Existential Anxiety and the Four Universal Concerns

Existential anxiety involves the experience of become aware of the human existential state of constant change (Cohn, 1993). Existential anxiety is a natural non-pathological concern, which is characteristic of all human beings. It is at the core of human existence and therefore is an essential ingredient of human consciousness. In other words, any human experience includes a relation to existential anxiety in one way or another; it is influenced by that anxiety and is shaped by it (Langdridge, 2013).

There are various approaches which aim to define universal concerns, the most common of which refer to death, freedom, isolation and meaning concerns. For example, the focus on the concern of death as the most salient factor influencing human psychology is discussed and operationalized in the Terror Management Theory (TMT) literature (Solomon et al., 2015); or Logotherapy's focus on meaning in life as developed by Viktor Frankl (Frankl, 1963).

Other approaches such as the Humanistic perspective include a wider spectrum of existential concerns, as reflected in the writings of Bugental (Bugental, 1981), Yalom (Yalom, 1980), and before them Rollo May (May, 1996). Yalom's approach in particular has become widely accepted, and the most representative among them (Temple & Gall, 2018). Given its centrality, it was chosen as a frame of reference to our discussion of existential anxiety.

According to Yalom's approach (Yalom, 1980), existential anxiety is comprised of four universal existential concerns.

The first aspect is expressed in the universal concern regarding **death** and the finality of life. It is a prominent aspect related to the experience of constant changing, transience and the finality of existence (e.g. Becker,

1973). Every experience of change is an experience of finality and death, in the sense that it is unrepeatable and cannot be relived in the same way again (Bugental, 1981). The authentic experience reminds the individual that any given moment is experienced in itself, while all the moments leading from it to the next are mere possibilities. One can only ever move forward, to the next choice, and not back.

Thus, the concern of death emerges from the experience of nothingness and the temporary nature of our existence (Wong, 2010).

The second concern is the concern of **freedom** and the guilt it may invoke in us. As Sartre's story about the French young man demonstrates, the choice between the mother and the nation involves guilt. The authentic experience involves a choice which determines the way in which reality is perceived and interpreted. Freedom embedded in the experience of groundlessness which may invoke guilt, given that any choice taken means that other options cease to exist (Bugental, 1981). In other words, every time we make a choice reality changes by omitting previous options and introducing brand new crossroads and potentials.

The third aspect of anxiety is reflected in the concern of **isolation**, which is another consequence of the experience of nothingness. This concern is embodied in the fact that as humans, we come into the world alone, and leave it the same way. Nobody, not even the closest people to us, can really understand our subjective experience first-hand. This experience of being alone at the center of our own world invokes the anxiety of isolation, and the pain of loneliness.

The fourth aspect is reflected in the concern of **meaninglessness**. Meaninglessness stems from the first three existential concerns, suggesting that if individuals are doomed to die, choose how to live their own lives, and remain ultimately alone, then what meaning is there to life? As Yalom (1980, p. 423) puts it: "human beings constitute themselves, their world, and their situation within that world… there exists no 'meaning,' no grand design in the universe, no guidelines for living other than those the individual creates".

In order to feel meaning in their lives, individuals need to self-transcend to face and encounter the outside world. Meaning is discovered in the intersubjective space in between subjective and objective. Only when a person experiences themselves as a part of reality, in possession of the power to influence it—they experience themselves as meaningful beings. Therefore, authentic people feel meaningful only when they co-create meaning in the reality of their world.

Taken together, the meaninglessness concern may yield **ongoing existential doubt and uncertainty** arising from the question: what for? Is there a meaning to a limited and temporary existence? (See Frankl, 1963).

As authentic existence involves the universal concerns and existential anxiety at the heart of human experience, most of us prefer to live in a state of forgetfulness-of-being. According to existential literature, in this state individuals deny their own Dasein consciousness, and prefer to live in self-deception, delusion, or false faith ('Bad Faith'; Sartre, 1956). These are designed to protect the individual against the difficulty of bearing the anxiety of existence in all its different variations.

Most of us cannot imagine ourselves existing without the 'voice in our head' which organizes and interprets reality for us in a logical, structured and clear way. It instructs us constantly how to behave, thus distinguishing us from the world around us. We are profoundly used to identifying ourselves with that 'voice in our head'. Therefore, the existential idea—that is, that our existence precedes our essence—is usually inconceivable.

We sink into forgetting that nothingness and groundlessness are fundamental ingredients to our experience of existence. We identify ourselves with that voice which always offers scripts and explanations for the world around us. Those explanations are based on familiar structures and patterns. We are convinced that the 'voice in our head' represents all that we are, and who we 'really' are. In fact, we prefer to live our life in accordance with the sound of the rational consciousness (Left Brain), which beyond its logical function also serves us as a calming and reassuring voice that enables us to live our daily life. We prefer to forget that the 'voice in our head' (our 'self') is only one interpretation of reality, merely one way to view it. It is the outcome of our experience and the socialization we were subjected to since childhood, by adults and social agents who taught us to think in a certain way about our experience.

Heidegger calls this state **inauthentic** existence (Heidegger, 1962), implying that we are not attentive to the pure absurd experience of Dasein, but only to a certain limited interpretation of it, one which we got used to over the years.

This means that most of us believe that there is a constant and stable 'self' that is clear and distinguished from its entire external social environment, that there is an eternal 'Somethingness' at the heart of the human entity, and that a universal set of rules navigates our life and takes care of our well-being. This false belief keeps at bay the possibility of experiencing the existential anxiety, the absurd. Thus, it maintains a sense of calmness and security. In this sense, there are many advantages to the inauthentic existence.

This issue also explains our difficulty in experiencing Dasein authentically, and the preference to live with split consciousness. The Dasein experience of being in the here and now might awaken the anxiety of existence and the absurd that lies within us. Therefore, we prefer to deny it, and live our lives inauthentically while protecting ourselves from the Dasein consciousness.

We do this by constantly distracting ourselves from the present moment to what will happen in the next, or to what already happened in the previous one. Alternatively, we do it by distracting ourselves from the experience of constant change regarding ourselves, the world and other people. And, in addition, by distracting ourselves from where we are in favor of where we have been, or where we will be.

The result, in either case, is the same: most people live their lives inauthentically. We prefer the inauthentic position that denies the Dasein experience (as in: 'this is how I've always been' or 'I have no choice'), in order to avoid the absurd and existential anxiety. Thus, we may sink into a comforting state of being forgetful of our own existence.

Authenticity and Neurotic Anxiety

A question arises, then. If authenticity, according to this approach, is awareness of existential anxiety, why should it be invoked? Considering that individuals wish to avoid the unsettling experience of anxiety, why should we encourage facing it?

The answer to these questions, according to existential psychology, is unequivocal. Mental health exists when one feels a certain extent of existential anxiety, which is, as noted, a natural human anxiety, and an indication of a life lived authentically. It is in fact our attempts to protect ourselves from existential anxiety and to eliminate its influence on our life, which invoke neurotic anxiety that may lead to psychological distress and suffering (Iacovou, 2011; May, 1996).

In other words, inauthentic experience involves an escape from the natural anxiety of existence. This may include the development of neurotic anxiety symptoms, and reported psychological distress. Neurotic anxiety is created in the inauthentic consciousness in an attempt to deflect and avoid existential anxiety.

There are two forms of neurotic anxiety. One is a denial of anxiety, as in 'there is no such thing'. At its radical end, it might cause depression and despair, because it leads to fixation and a reduction of vitality to an extent of stagnation. This type of neurotic anxiety can be viewed as avoiding existential anxiety, because it is focused on the negative aspects of anxiety and attempts to deny it (Bugental, 1981; Greening, 1992).

A second form evolves out of accepting the existential anxiety, while the purpose of the defense mechanism is to constantly overcome it. In other words, it aims to deflect the anxiety by sinking into endless neurotic action in order to 'avoid thinking about it' and also to 'prove it wrong'. This type of neurotic anxiety can be seen as an attempt to win the battle against existential anxiety by creating a pretense that it can be defeated (Greening, 1992; Bugental, 1981). Generally, we refer to those two defense mechanisms as denial defense mechanism and neurotic defense mechanism, respectively.

According to the thinkers who have laid the foundations for Existential psychology (such as Heidegger, 1962), people experience their life in one of two ways. The first is authentically, that is, in awareness of existential anxiety. The second is inauthentically, that is, while defending oneself from what is seen as neurotic anxiety. Nowadays, it is less common to view 'authenticity' as a completely opposite and distinguished state from 'inauthenticity'. The second-generation thinkers of the existential school tend to realize that it is, in fact, impossible to be authentic all the time. They suggest that authenticity and inauthenticity are better thought of as a spectrum, rather than as two separate states of being (e.g. Pollard, 2005; Van-Deurzen-Smith, 1997). In other words, authenticity can be increased, but there will always be an extent of inauthenticity in our life. According to this approach, the right amount of anxiety leads to encountering and living a more authentic life, hence a more meaningful existence with a greater amount of mental health (Bugental, 1981; Greening, 1992) (See Fig. 3.1).

In sum, authenticity is the measure of mindfulness and acceptance of the Dasein experience. The more such mindfulness exists, the more an individual is aware of the nothingness, temporality, and groundlessness at the core of their being. They are therefore more exposed to encountering the four universal concerns that such condition may invoke. Authenticity is an awareness of the human freedom to choose how to experience reality, and all that comes with it, existential anxiety included. Denial of existential anxiety would invoke neurotic anxiety and various defense mechanisms aiming to deflect it. We shall now take a closer look at each of the existential concerns, and their related defense mechanisms (denial or neurotic).

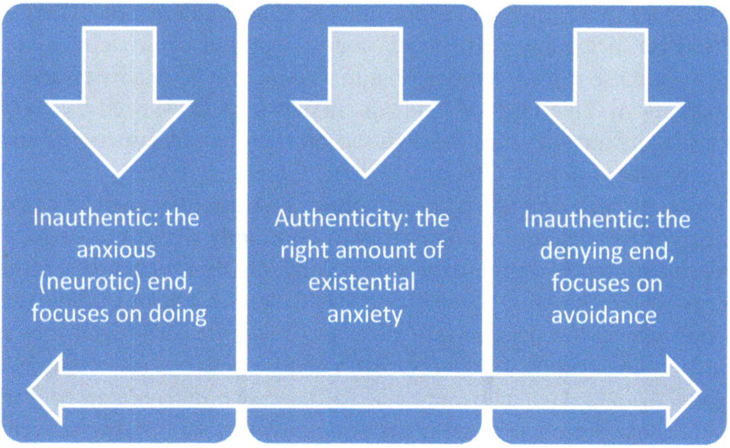

Fig. 3.1 Authenticity and inauthenticity as a range

The Universal Concern of Death

As previously discussed, the authentic individual is aware of the temporality and nothingness at the core of their being which involves the existential concern of death and annihilation. This concern accompanies us from the beginning of our life. Newborns feel it in the sense of lack of objects' permanence (Winnicott, 1958), namely the fact that babies cannot grasp the fact that objects keep existing even when they are out of their sight.

Thus, when the baby experiences their mother in their field of perception—they calm down. But when the mother leaves the room, the 'abandoned' baby feels the anxiety of death. In the baby's perception, once the mother left their realm of perception—she is out of their world's experience, and there is no telling whether she is ever coming back.

Consider the baby's perspective as an experience of instability and constant change, where we cannot be sure whether the object we currently experience would exist (rematerialize) in the next moment. This phenomenon sustains until the baby learns about the permanence of objects. Namely, their rational brain functions develop, and they can come to the realization that even when they do not experience a certain object (e.g. the mother), it still exists unrelated to their experience.

However, the construct of 'death' as absence already exists, and it expresses itself through various manifestations in different developmental stages. It forever accompanies the individual like a shadow at the fringes of consciousness. It symbolizes the fear of change, loss, and reality's instability. In the early developmental stages of childhood (from the age of 6) until early adulthood (age 25–30), other life tasks take central stage. For example, academic success and skill development in childhood; shaping a mature identity during adolescence, finding a spouse and forging a professional career and identity later in life, and so on (on tasks and developmental stages throughout the life course see Erikson, 1994).

Between the ages of 30 and 50, death consciousness returns to occupy a more central place. It is enhanced especially around what is known as the midlife crisis, which brings to the surface existential issues, and the transience of life. Death consciousness may appear regardless of age, in the context of life crises such as a loss of a significant person, or more global crises such as war or plague. Sometimes it is more pronounced, while at other times it tends to appear clandestine, rooted in the lived experience of finality, vulnerability, mortality, and failure.

Why a black shadow? At the heart of the death consciousness stands, for most people, the main anxiety deriving from their own mortality—Death anxiety (Bugental, 1981). Namely, most people do not accept serenely the fact of their own inevitable demise, as this fact brings with it anxiety and distress. In fact, we find in literature, poetry, folk tales, and religious traditions various ways of dealing with the human concern of death. Among those mechanisms are the beliefs in an after-life, reincarnation, eternity of the soul, and so on. All are attempts to dismiss the mightiness of the anxiety, and the very existence of death. One of the ideas often mentioned by contemporary scholars (Harari, 2016) is that death is humans' ultimate nemesis, while humanity's deep interest in technology is rooted in the hope that we might be able to eliminate death, or at least delay it for as long as possible.

We shall now examine the defense mechanisms accompanying the fear of death. Such defense mechanisms range from neurotic defenses where individuals go about their life obsessively, with an awareness of their mortality (a 'death exists' position) to denial defenses, where individuals develop fixations, rituals and ceremonies aiming to keep anxiety at bay and to dismiss its influence (a 'there is no death' position) (Greening, 1992; Yalom, 1980).

Neurotic defense mechanisms against the death concern may include (among others)—a pessimistic approach to life, neurotic disorders such as self-sabotage, addictive and obsessive behaviors, sexually acting out, infidelity, and engagement with risky or workaholic behaviors. Other options may include the development of a sense of fatalism, suicidal tendencies, accident prone tendencies, health neglect, and proclivity to invest excessive time in rituals. Sometimes there may be a proclivity to engage in dangerous and extreme sports or other forms of activities in order to eliminate anxiety and reinforce a sense of lack of vulnerability. Such defenses generally invoke a tendency to stimulate a sense of overcoming death (Greening, 1992; Yalom, 1980).

Denial based defense mechanisms against the death concern may include (among others)—A tendency to deny the very existence of death or that it can influence one's life may include displacement, suppression, repression, belief in personal omnipotence and invulnerability. It may also involve acceptance of socially sanctioned religious beliefs that reframe death, or personal efforts to overcome death through achieving symbolic immortality. Such defenses may also stimulate grandiosity and a sense of mightiness and perpetuity of body or soul refusal to acknowledge the finality of life and a delusion of no vulnerability. There is often a sanctifying of youth, health, beauty and sensuality, hedonism and debauchery, and a tendency to be powerful and to control the reality of life. Also common are willingness to be aggressive and the display of sexual behavior that may be promiscuous. All of these behaviors are based on a premise that pushes the fear of death away and assumes that 'this will not happen to me' (Greening, 1992; Yalom, 1980).

All of the defenses may lead to an inauthentic existence, where individuals try to shake off their authentic existence and indulge in forgetfulness of being, which keeps the death concern away.

Alongside these aspects, researchers and scholars have also indicated the potential positive influences of encountering death as part of life, especially with regard to our sense of vitality and creativity (Bugental, 1981; Greening, 1992). Without death, we wouldn't be able to feel the urge to change our lives and our personalities. In this context, Yalom (Yalom, 1980, p. 7) argues that, "The physicality of death destroys us; the idea of death saves us". In other words, while physical death terminates us, the idea that we are about to die rescues us. It does so in the sense that it plants within us all that is moral. Through the fear, we understand the pain and anxiety of other beings and are capable of developing compassion and empathy for all that is around us. Therefore, the authentic position regarding the concern of death is one that learns to live with this anxiety without attempting to eliminate it in one way or another.

In summary, positive effects of an authentic perception of death may include—the ability to celebrate the different phases of life even when they involve issues of endings, loss, and letting go (e.g. when grown up children leave the family nest). Such ability goes hand in hand with coming to terms with our mortality. It means being able to choose to live fully and to experience the beauty in life despite an acknowledgemnt of its fragility and finitude (Bugental, 1981; Greening, 1992).

An authentic encounter with the right dose of the idea of death may be impactful in leading to a change in our self-perception and world view. In some cultures, a part of the process of initiation and coming of age includes a symbolic 'death' of the child (or the previous developmental stage) so that they may regrow as adults (Lévi-Strauss, 2013). The right dose is the authentic state of awareness to existential anxiety, where there is a balance between neurosis and denial. It is embodied in the acceptance of the finality of death and coming to terms with the infinite changing of life.

A moment for thought: The concern of death. Think about a moment in which you have encountered the concern of death in your life. What happened? How did the consciousness of death arise and what change had it generated in you (remember that the concern of death is a part of the authentic consciousness, and therefore is always related to change)? What can be learned from this experience that is applicable to your life today?

The Universal Concern of Freedom

In the first chapter of this book, we discussed the freedom concern at length. We saw that the authentic state involves being aware of a sense of groundlessness, and that freedom means making choices without knowing for certain where they lead. An important aspect of this is the anxiety that accompanies this act of choice, and the guilt involved in deciding how one wishes to live in the world (May, 1994). Every choice means eliminating other choices. For example, if you have chosen to be a parent, you cannot go back to being childless, namely, you have irrevocably altered your status in the world and life experience.

Every existential choice embodies a constant change in an individual's status in the world, and therefore it invokes guilt. This is because there will always be voices telling us that we should have chosen otherwise. Whichever route we choose—we will always feel guilt and regret about the road unchosen (Bugental, 1981). In modern terms, we may refer to this as reflected in the FOMO, the Fear of Missing Out phenomenon (Milyavskaya et al., 2018). If we go back to Sartre's young Frenchman example—if he opts to stay with his mother— he might feel as if the blood of his friends who die at war will forever be on his hands; but if he chooses to go to war and join them—he might feel guilty for his mother's death. There is no easy choice. An existential choice is in essence difficult and challenging, and it always carries with it an immense guilt anxiety.

In order to deal with the guilt anxiety, individuals may develop defenses. Here, too, there is a range of defenses, from the neurotic to denial based. The neurotic defenses assume that freedom exists, and therefore the individual bears responsibility and guilt for all the consequences of their actions, that is, an internal locus of control. As a result, people develop a defensive guilt as in 'I am always to blame'. They do so in order to regain a sense of control and security on the one hand, or a belief in bigger powers of fate that take away that freedom and eliminate it—on the other.

Neurotic defenses against the Freedom concern and the anxiety of guilt include, among others—an illusion of control that may include internal locus of control, defensive guilt, compulsivity, irrational behavior, excessive eating or shopping behavior, and espousing fatalistic worldviews or superstitions (e.g. Carlson et al., 2009; Yalom, 1980). Furthermore, in some cases it may involve self-enslavement, dependency, submission to 'tyrants', gurus, and powerful people, and addiction to drugs or alcohol. In other cases, scientific determinism may be invoked—namely believing that everything in nature takes place according to a programmed set of rules (see, e.g. Yalom, 1980).

On the other hand, there are defenses which deny guilt and enable a sense of escape from taking responsibility. Such is the false belief presented by Sartre (Sartre, 1956), in which individuals justify their behavior with "I do not have a choice, because …", or an external locus of control. This defense actually enables a worry-free existence, while focusing on self-serving needs of the individual without bringing others, or the social cultural environment surrounding the individual, into account.

Defense mechanisms that deny the Freedom concern include, among other things—A sense of freedom without boundaries or **responsibility**, self-expression at all costs while ignoring other people's needs, social systems, or physical limitations. It may involve turning the self-fulfillment value into a 'religion' or guiding ideology, without any consideration for others who might pay the price for it (Greening, 1992). What all those defenses have in common is that they may lead to inauthentic existence in which an individual attempts to shake their freedom consciousness off. Then, they may sink into forgetfulness of being which keeps the anxiety of guilt away.

In contrast, the authentic position towards freedom is one that takes responsibility for one's choices, as in "my way is the moral person's way" (Levinas, 2019). Assuming responsibility means bearing an existential guilt, which is a balancing act between denying guilt to accepting it in a defensive way.

As seen in Sartre's young Frenchman's example, this is the only way to feel integrity and morality in a world devoid of absolute values of right and wrong (Sartre, 1956), and as such it may carry a positive influence on individuals. Beyond establishing a sense of integrity, responsibility also creates unity between the various parts of the personality, and inner crystallization within it (Yalom, 1980).

A moment for thought: the Freedom concern. Think of a moment in which you have encountered the Freedom concern in your life. What were the circumstances? What happened? How was the concern of Freedom triggered and what change did it generate in your life? (Remember, the freedom concern is a part of the authentic consciousness and is therefore always related to change.)

The Universal Concern of Isolation

Similar to the death concern, the isolation concern too floats at the fringes of our consciousness. It moves into the center of awareness when individuals are in radical states, and feel their isolation vis-à-vis the world in the sense that nobody in the whole world understands their feeling and situation as they view and experience it subjectively.

Human beings are born alone and die alone, and can never share those experiences with others. Such experience of isolation is not reflected only in birth or death; humans encounter their isolation whenever they become conscious to the fact that no one can really understand what it means to be 'in their skin' and to see things the way they see it.

When an individual encounters their isolation, they may feel pain for the inability to exceed this sense of existential loneliness. It may make them feel more sensitive, vulnerable, and exposed, because at the core of their existence, there is an anxiety-inducing nothingness which they must hide from others. Even the closest people to us cannot fully grasp our experience.

This isolation anxiety has an effect on us, both inward and outward. Inward effect is directed toward the self, namely, intrapersonal, and outward effect is directed toward others, namely, interpersonal. The intrapersonal isolation means feeling self-alienation and a split between different aspects and parts of the self that do not get expressed (e.g. being alienated to the need to be successful, be loved, be curious, etc.). Interpersonal isolation implies limited social abilities, and difficulties in having and maintaining intimate relationships with significant others (e.g. Rogers, 1980; Yalom, 1980).

A set of defenses is developed in order to avoid the Isolation anxiety. Those, too, range between neurotic defenses aiming to escape isolation by being in constant action; to denial defenses, attempting to elude isolation by denying it. On the one end of the spectrum, we can find defenses which reflect the belief that 'there is isolation' and aim to shield oneself from the outside world.

Neurotic defenses typical to the isolation concern and the tendency toward detachment may include—misanthropy, nurturing an abstinent and lonesome lifestyle, condescending and a-social behavior as a way to avoid human contact, developing a rationalizing philosophical system to justify values of solitude and using other people as objects to satisfy needs rather than treat them as subjects with their own will and emotions. Alternatively, angry and begrudging behavior toward others, unforgiving at all costs—are all used as a strategy to keep others away and avoid intimacy (Greening, 1992).

On the other end of the spectrum, we can find denying defense mechanisms of isolation, reflecting the belief that 'there is no isolation'. This kind of defenses is represented by an inclination to 'fusion' with others in order to produce an experience of self-disregard and ignoring or belittling the isolation experience (under the assumption that if there is no distinguishable 'self'—there is no isolation).

Typical defenses for denial of isolation and the proclivity for symbiosis may include—conformism, a constant need for recognition and validation from others, self-scarifying of one's own needs in favor of others. Other behaviors may involve over-engagement in socialization to avoid being alone. Alternatively, it can manifest in a need to belong to an identity group (e.g., family, organization, community, economic entity etc.), and generally—a strong need to be a part of a 'herd' or a pack, and identify oneself through such affiliation (Greening, 1992).

Overall, the defenses against the isolation anxiety aim to shield the individual from experiencing the painful side of their existential isolation. The authentic consciousness enables the individual to feel the pain of loneliness, and share it—with themselves, and then with others. Therefore, authentic isolation may have a positive influence. The ability to be exposed and vulnerable when facing reality and others, at the right measure, enables us to develop intimacy with ourselves, with other people around us, and with a community, or other reference groups. This intimacy, in turn, is the basis for authentic love (see Fromm, 2000).

A moment for thought: the Isolation concern. Think about a moment in your life in which you have encountered the isolation concern. What were the circumstances? What happened? How did the isolation concern arise and what change has it generated in your life? (Remember, Isolation concern is part of the authentic consciousness; therefore, it is always related to change).

The Universal Concern of Meaninglessness

This concern is often perceived as more fundamental than the previously mentioned three (Frankl, 1963). In fact, it is the meaninglessness concern that kick-started existential thinking when Friedrich Nietzsche (e.g. Nietzsche, 2005) pondered in his philosophical writing about the changes in the modern world. He observed that it was moving further away from dogmatic religious thinking which offers a certain kind of meaning and direction to life, toward establishing human knowledge and growth upon rational and logical thinking at the center.

The problem that Nietzsche identified, and preoccupied many of his contemporaries in literature, arts, poetry, and philosophy—is one of morals and human behavior. If there is no God, no one truth, no clear meaning to life—then morals and binding values are all thrown into the dustbin of history. Because, in this new world, every individual is free to live as they chose and still feel morally virtuous and just. In other words, morals are only relative, not universal.

Nietzsche realized that the main anxiety behind the lack of morality is the Meaninglessness concern and the nihilism it may inflict on– namely denying reality and bringing about an 'each to their own' approach. At the basis of this concern lies a chilling, almost unbearable uncertainty. It is the uncertainty that is at the core of human isolation, freedom (groundlessness), the anxiety of death, and the finality of the individual.

It implies that there is no purpose to our existence, that we exist with no reason or meaning; and that therefore the only solution for our existential condition is to delve into existential depression. The concern of meaninglessness is, then, a source of existential anxiety which sips through the existential state of the individual. It is present in all human thoughts and actions, whatever they may be. At the heart of this concern are the unanswered questions regarding the meaning in one's life (what has meaning in my life? what is valuable to me?) and the meaning of life in general (is there a meaning to life in general?).

As the concern of meaninglessness and the uncertainty which accompanies it are unbearable, a wide range of defense mechanisms aiming to shield individuals from this concern may evolve. Such defenses range from neurotic to denial based. The neurotic aspect of the defense ('ameaning exists and it is clear') includes committing oneself to one truth which gives life a sturdy, even rigid, meaning. Accordingly, this involves an attempt to gain strict control over reality, and to grant life a meaning-affirming framework as a defense against uncertainty.

Typical neurotic defenses for the Meaninglessness concern and the uncertainty anxiety may include—a radical faith in a certain religion or in science, fanaticisms, total loyalty to a leader or social institution, or a proclivity toward radicalism, fundamentalism, totalitarianism, or hedonism. Sometimes it may involve a tendency for delinquency and obsessive behaviors (e.g. Frankl, 1963; Wong, 2010).

On the other end of the spectrum, there are denial-based defenses that embrace the meaninglessness anxiety while completely relinquishing control. Such defenses may lead to sinking into the existential vacuum and the depression shrouding this position.

Typical denial-based defenses against the Meaninglessness concern and the uncertainty anxiety may include—nihilism, existential void or vacuum, boredom, apathy, belief in a chaotic and meaningless universe, and hedonism. The latter may lead to rejecting all sacred social and cultural values, and eventually plummeting into emptiness and depression (Wong, 2010).

What the different defenses, neurotic and denial based alike, have in common is that they numb individuals from being in contact with and experiencing the meaninglessness, void, and uncertainty. Thus, they create an inauthentic existence in which individuals sink in forgetfulness of being.

Nietzsche (2005) suggested that the existential nothingness or void involved with a sense of meaninglessness and uncertainty leaves the individual with two alternatives:

1. To sink into depression because of the meaninglessness of existence and the existential depression engulfing it.
2. To create a new value-based reality which is unique for the individual—one that makes them an active agent and participant who has full responsibility for their existence.

Nietzsche advocated for the second alternative, namely avoiding a passive approach and aligning oneself to face nothingness through an active approach. Meaninglessness should be considered as an invitation to individuals to be active partners in constructing the social world they choose to live in. According to Nietzsche, living in a world where the individual is an active player in forming reality is a meaningful and worthy way of living. Such involvement requires responsibility, but it also grants them the satisfaction in their creation and more meaningful involvement in their life.

A similar idea is expressed in the Old Testament story of Job. The book tells of a man named Job who loses all his property and his beloved family in a series of catastrophes that befall him as a result of a provocation set at God by Satan. Satan seeks to prove to God that Job is upright only because he is happy. If Job suffers, claims Satan, his virtuousness will be compromised too. Thus, Job is hit by terrible calamities, and he gradually loses all he had. Job's friends get together and try to seek meaning in his predicament. They offer several responses, to Job's situation:

1. The catastrophes derive from Job's sins (despite his righteous reputation); they are a punishment aiming to purify him. The suffering befalls the sinner to mend their ways. The bottom line is that Job is to blame for his downfall. Job rejects this argument.

2. The world is a bad place (as in: 'the righteous suffer'). This is the world's nature and it can't be helped. This idea, too, is rejected by Job.
3. The calamities' objective is to turn Job into a better man; namely, the bad in our life aims to improve it, therefor it is a part of the good. Job disagrees with this explanation, too.
4. Finally comes a fourth reasoning, which seems to come from God's mouth: humans cannot understand the meaning of existence. Therefore, all they can do is be **active participants, to be committed to their** reality, and to **seek meaning** in all that they do, without reaching a position of complete understanding of one's overall life or existence. According to this approach, Job will never be able to understand why all those catastrophes have befallen him. Therefore, he will always live in existential doubt. All he can do is keep striving to actively participate and commit to his reality as it is revealed to him. He should believe that it involves clandestine meaning which he must keep seeking for, and discover. The encounter between the human will and the existing reality—is the bedrock on which meaning grows. There is no ruling as to whether reality is good or bad, as it is a choice. There is only a constant search and a relentless effort toward active participation that yields existential meaning.

This idea of seeking meaning through active participation in life and the external world connects to what Sartre (2007), as well as Levinas (e.g. Levinas, 2019), referred to as integrity. Only an individual who opts to be an active participant in co-creating his or her experience and in discovering meaning can experience integrity, that is, co-create the reality in which they want to live in.

Going back to Sartre's example (2007), it is impossible to determine what is more important: collective or personal values. Therefore, an individual can never be able to know for certain whether their behavior in a certain situation (e.g., choosing between the mother and the nation) was right or wrong. They can only know they have done the best they could in given circumstances. In aiming toward active co-participation with and **commitment** to the circumstances that occurred, they are be able to build a joint reality in which they want to live and in which they feel meaningful.

In other words, there is a positive aspect to the authentic encounter with the concern of meaninglessness. The more an individual labors to actively commit to the reality in which they live in, the more they are aware of the natural and existential concerns of life. And then, they can act out of an authentic position regarding their reality. They can operate out of acceptance of their own mortality, taking responsibility over their choices. They are able to create intimate and close relationships with their close environment. All of this, together and separately, increase the sense of life's meaning (Vos, 2015).

The concern of Meaninglessness can be identified as the most basic of the universal concerns. Logotherapy (meaning-centered psychotherapy), created by the psychiatrist and neurologist Viktor Frankl, is the main approach tying psychotherapy to meaning in life. According to Logotherapy (Frankl, 1969), meaning can be found via three main pathways:

Creation—what we give to the world in terms of accomplishing a task, creating a work, or making a contribution. This may include involvement in doing, creating, giving through work that expresses our unique fingertip or "traces" in the world.

Experience—what we take from the world in terms of experiencing beauty, art, nature, and significant relationships with others.

Attitude or taking a stand—how we relate and respond to what happens to us, especially to the things we cannot change or control, such as unavoidable suffering.

Beyond experiencing and creating, our position is particularly important at times of crisis, strife, and suffering. In such circumstances, the individual can find meaning in life thanks to their stand or approach. This process which sometimes requires time and processing may yield new insights and opportunities to evolve, discover new meanings, and grow from the challenge, as can be seen for example in accounts of post-traumatic growth (PTG). In other words, it can turn a personal tragedy into a human victory. Those three routes reflect the individual's authentic ability to be involved in life and self-transcend toward a worthy goal.

A moment for thought: the meaninglessness concern. Think about a moment in which you have encountered Meaninglessness in your life. What were the circumstances? What happened? How did this concern arise and what change did it generate in your life? (Remember, the meaninglessness concern is a part of the authentic consciousness and is therefore always related to change.)

Table 3.1 Existential concerns defense mechanisms and the authentic experience

Existential Concern	*Dominant anxiety*	*Neurotic-based defense*	*Being authentic*	*Denial-based defense*
Death	Death anxiety, fear of mortality, finality and failure	Obsession ('there is death')	**Existential anxiety: Accepting death and coming to terms with it**	Illusion of invincibility ('there is no death')
Freedom	Guilt anxiety,	Defensive guilt, internal locus of control ('there is guilt')	**Existential guilt: Taking responsibility**	Denial of responsibility, external locus of control ('there is no guilt')
Isolation	Loneliness anxiety, fear of shame and exposure	Social isolation and a-social stance ('there is isolation')	**Intimacy and vulnerability: Being exposed**	Conformism ('there is no isolation')
Meaninglessness	Meaninglessness anxiety, fear of uncertainty	Radicalism and control ('there is one clear meaning/ everything is meaningful')	**Being in existential doubt: Active participation, commitment**	Existential vacuum, nihilism and hedonism ('there is no meaning')

The following table presents existential concerns and their related defense mechanisms (Table 3.1).

Authenticity and Psychotherapy

Authenticity has a special value in psychotherapeutic treatment. The right (natural) amount of anxiety enables change in the essence of an individual's life and their self-perception, and bestows well-being. In general, it can be claimed that a person who turns to therapy does it because they are in distress and wish to deal with it. The different types of therapy offer a variety of responses to distress. In the existential approach, the focus is on the encounter with the individual's authentic consciousness that is enables to deal with challenges and suffering. An authentic encounter would enable the individual to see other interpretations for their life's circumstances, and also to identify a meaningful path for him or her to follow. On this basis they can change the direction and essence of their life (the 'self'), and experience life differently (van Deurzen, 2002).

For this reason, existentialists aspire to stimulate individuals to be aware of their existential anxiety and to regulate it (i.e., the authentic stance), so that they will become aware of their situational freedom and could opt to live their life in a more meaningful way (Bugental, 1981). Thus, the heart of existential therapy is in regulating anxiety to the right level, between neurotic defenses and denial-based ones. The purpose is to increase authentic consciousness of change in order to strengthen the ability to choose to live differently in the world. The aim of the therapeutic process is to broaden the client's range of possibilities in relation to their situation in life and their circumstances, and then to reduce anxiety so that they can identify the meaningful path for them to follow in life.

In fact, even if after the therapeutic process the client opts to keep living as they did prior to the intervention, they'll be doing so from an authentic position, rather than due to a false belief that they 'have no choice'. This is the difference between living authentic lives, aware of choices taken and assuming responsibility for them—and living inauthentically, with no awareness of one's freedom and no ability to change life circumstances even if the desire to do so exists. In this sense, existential therapy and its relation to authenticity resonate with the old symbol of medicine (see Fig. 3.2).

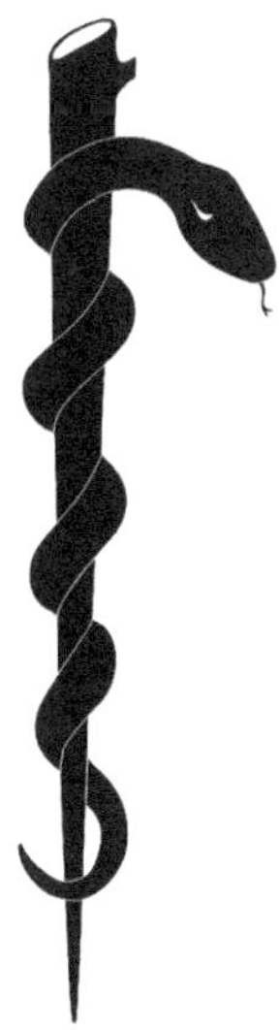

Fig. 3.2 The symbol of medicine

The ancient symbol of medicine displays a serpent wrapped around a staff. The staff was a sign of old age in the ancient world because elderly people typically used it as a walking aid. Old age was also a sign of wisdom. The snake manifests the poison in its teeth. What is the connection between the two?

Even in the olden days, it was common knowledge that a cure for an illness depends on the right dosage. This implied that a medication given in the wrong dose might harm or even kill—like the snake's poison. Thus, the snake is wrapped around the staff of old age to imply that curing is the wisdom of converting poison into medicine. In other words, the right dose of a medicine heals, while a misuse of any medicine might kill.

The same goes for using anxiety in existential therapy: the right extent connects the individual to an authentic and more meaningful existence, and may generate a significant and valuable change. However, a wrong dose of anxiety would bring about more damage than benefit. In this context, a crucial question emerges: what is the right dose of anxiety? How do we manage an individual's anxiety to just the right amount? Or, more generally: **how is existential thinking implemented in psychotherapy?**

References

Becker, E. (1973). *The denial of death.* Free Press.

Bugental, J. F. (1981). *The search for authenticity: An existential-analytic approach to psychotherapy.* Irvington Pub.

Carlson, B. D., Mowen, J. C., & Fang, X. (2009). Trait superstition and consumer behavior: Re-conceptualization, measurement, and initial investigations. *Psychology & Marketing, 26*(8), 689–713. https://doi.org/10.1002/mar.20295

Cohn, H. W. (1993). Authenticity and the aims of psychotherapy. *Journal of the society for existential analysis., 4*, 48–56.

Erikson, E. H. (1994). *Identity and the life cycle.* WW Norton & Company.

Frankl, V. (1949/1963). *Man's search for meaning: An introduction to logotherapy.* Pocket Books.

Frankl, V. (1969). Reduction and nihilism. In A. Koestler & J. R. Smythies (Eds.), *Beyond reductionism.* Beacon Press.

Fromm, E. (2000). *The art of loving: The centennial edition.* A&C Black.

Golomb, J. (2012). *In search of authenticity: Existentialism from Kierkegaard to Camus.* Routledge.

Greening, T. (1992). Existential challenges and responses. *The Humanistic Psychologist, 20*(1), 111.

Harari, Y. N. (2016). *Homo Deus: A brief history of tomorrow*. Random House.
Heidegger, M. (1962). *Being and time* (J. Macquarrie & E. Robinson, Trans.). Blackwell.
Iacovou, S. (2011). What is the difference between existential anxiety and so called neurotic anxiety? *Existential Analysis: Journal of the Society for Existential Analysis, 22*(2).
Ilies, R., Morgeson, F. P., & Nahrgang, J. D. (2005). Authentic leadership and eudemonic well-being: Understanding leader–follower outcomes. *The Leadership Quarterly, 16*(3), 373–394.
James, W. (1902/1958). *Varieties of religious experience*. Mentor.
Kierkegaard, S. (2013). *Fear and trembling and the sickness unto death*. Princeton University Press.
Lakey, C. E., Kernis, M. H., Heppner, W. L., & Lance, C. E. (2008). Individual differences in authenticity and mindfulness as predictors of verbal defensiveness. *Journal of Research in Personality, 42*(1), 230–238.
Langdridge, D. (2013). *Existential counselling & psychotherapy*. Sage.
Levinas, E. (2019). *Nine talmudic readings*. Indiana University Press.
Lévi-Strauss, C. (2013). *Myth and meaning*. Routledge.
May, R. (1994). Contributions of existential psychotherapy. In R. May, E. Angel, & H. F. Ellenberger (Eds.), *Existence* (pp. 37–92). Jason Aronson.
May, R. (1996). *The meaning of anxiety*. WW Norton & Company.
Milyavskaya, M., Saffran, M., Hope, N., & Koestner, R. (2018). Fear of missing out: Prevalence, dynamics, and consequences of experiencing FOMO. *Motivation and Emotion, 42*(5), 725–737.
Nietzsche, F. W. (2005). *Thus spoke Zarathustra: A book for everyone and nobody*. Oxford University Press.
Pollard, J. O. H. N. (2005). Authenticity and inauthenticity. *Existential Perspectives On human Issues: A Handbook for Therapeutic Practice*, 171–179.
Rogers, C. (1980). *A way of being*. Houghton Mifflin.
Ryan, W. S., & Ryan, R. M. (2019). Toward a social psychology of authenticity: Exploring within-person variation in autonomy, congruence, and genuineness using self-determination theory. *Review of General Psychology, 23*(1), 99–112.
Sartre, J. P. (2007). *Existentialism is a humanism* (C. Macomber, Trans.). Yale University Press.
Sartre, J.-P. (1956). *Being and nothingness: An essay in phenomenological ontology* (H. E. Barnes, Trans.). Philosophical Library.
Schlegel, R. J., Hicks, J. A., Arndt, J. A., & King, L. A. (2011). Feeling like you know who you are: Perceived true self-knowledge and meaning in life. *Personality and Social Psychological Bulletin, 37*, 745–756.
Solomon, S., Greenberg, J., & Pyszczynski, T. (2015). *The worm at the core: On the role of death in life*. Random House.

Temple, M., & Gall, T. L. (2018). Working through existential anxiety toward authenticity: A spiritual journey of meaning making. *Journal of Humanistic Psychology, 58*(2), 168–193.

van Deurzen, E. (2002). *Existential counselling in practice.* Sage.

Van-Deurzen-Smith, E. (1997). *Everyday mysteries.* Routledge.

Vos, J. (2015). Meaning and existential givens in the lives of cancer patients: A philosophical perspective on psycho-oncology. *Palliative & Supportive Care, 13*(4), 885.

Winnicott, D. W. (1958). The capacity to be alone. *International Journal of Psychoanalysis, 39*, 416–420.

Winnicott, D. W. (2018). Ego distortion in terms of true and false self. In *The person who is me* (pp. 7–22). Routledge.

Wong, P. T. P. (2010). What is existential positive psychology? *International journal of existential psychology & psychotherapy, 3*(1), 1–10.

Yalom, I. D. (1980). *Existential psychotherapy.* Basic Books.

PART II

Applications

CHAPTER 4

The Therapeutic Model

Abstract This chapter introduces the phenomenological-existential approach to psychotherapy and intervention. It begins with a comparison between two models of care—deficit-correction and understanding-collaboration—and explains the use and implementation of each according to various psychological perspectives, including the psychodynamic and the cognitive. The chapter differentiates the phenomenological-existential therapeutic approach from other psychotherapeutic perspectives, particularly as to how it advocates intervention with no predefined therapeutic goals, in order to preserve the importance of the subjective experience and the uniqueness of the individual.

Keywords The therapeutic model • The 'deficit-corrective' model • The 'understanding-collaboration' model • Dynamic approach • Cognitive approach • Existential approach

This part of the book describes the practice of using existential thinking. It can be read in two ways—specifically for clinical work, or more generally for individual self-work in the context of nurturing one's authentic experience, in order to increase one's own situational freedom and develop their sense of meaning in life.

J. Davidov, P. Russo-Netzer, *Existential Authenticity*,
https://doi.org/10.1007/978-3-031-07842-2_4

The human experience of freedom raises fundamental questions in the context of psychotherapy. The first one that comes to mind is how to establish therapeutic intervention based on the idea of rejecting universal values of what is right or wrong for people's well-being. This rejection stands in contrast with having a set of guiding 'therapeutic values and aims', most therapists engage with in their clinical practice and intervention.

For example, an accepted guiding principle may be that depression is 'bad' and should be treated, just as trauma is 'bad' and should be 'fixed'. Furthermore, the very definition of this therapeutic realm as 'mental health' implies that 'mental illness' is something that one should be 'healed' from. In the very least, it is assumed that one should learn to deal with and 'live with' it, in a way that would not harm them or cause excessive suffering.

It can be carefully asserted that Western society had placed the term 'normative' at the center of the therapeutic discourse. This involves a clear infrastructure of values and aims—being 'normative' is good; being 'non-normative' is bad. Based on that, most classical therapeutic models were offered to 'fix' what causes the client's suffering. It is important to note that nowadays there are different integrative schools, combining classic approaches with varied therapeutic methods and a multitude of orientations to confront human psychological suffering and distress.

Within this range, Existential psychology stands out for putting the idea of freedom at the center of its discipline. This is a notion that practically rejects absolute ideas or values of 'right' or 'wrong', 'good' or 'bad'. Therefore, the question is how we create a therapeutic model without such universal guiding values, without a 'good' versus a 'bad', that requires amending.

This chapter compares different therapeutic approaches, in particular the deficit-corrective therapeutic model and the understanding-collaboration therapeutic model that is more typical to Existential psychology. We note that in existential thinking, there is no 'normative' realm of human behavior, nor can there be. Each and every one of us is an individual human project in our own right. On this premise, we suggest a therapeutic model that refrains from trying to impose predetermined values of 'health' versus 'illness'. Rather, it aims to help the free individual to deal with the challenges stopping him or her from encountering and fulfilling their full potential, so that they could live what they perceive as a full and meaningful life.

A 'Deficit-Corrective' Model Compared to an 'Understanding-Collaboration' Model of Psychotherapy

First, we discuss the 'corrective' model, widely known as the 'deficit-correction' model. It aims to treat, correct, and improve the psychological state of an individual (e.g., Dubose, 2015). Roughly, the premise of the model is that the suffering of an individual who seeks therapy derives from a 'less adequate' way of life. It therefore assumes that there is a 'better' way of living.

This therapeutic model is often embodied by the two classical schools of therapy—the Psychodynamic and the Cognitive. We shall hereby explain how each of those approaches establishes a corrective model.

The Dynamic Approach—The Conflict at the Basis of the Personality

In the Dynamic approach, the main term characterizing the psychological structure of the individual is the assumed existence of a 'personality' as an undeniable axiom. The personality is the arena in which two central forces generating human consciousness meet: the Eros (the urge for life, or life instinct, which includes the libido) and the Thanatos (the urge of death, or death instinct). Both powers are in constant conflict, and the meeting and equilibrium point (homeostasis) between them influences the individual's interpretation of reality.

This conflict has a dynamic that can be characterized using various models including, among others, the Topographic model (conscious/subconscious/unconscious); the Structural model (Id/Ego/Superego); the Genital model (oral/anal/phallic/latent/genital), the Psycho-Social (which lines up eight developmental stages) and others.

The dynamics of the conflict explains the individual's behavior in the reality of their life. The Genital model, for example, assumes that the personality has a few developmental stages that are related to the individual's biological age. They bear far reaching implications on behavior in the course of one's life. If the person's needs are provided, their personality learns at the different stages of development that the world can be trusted (the Oral phase), that it has will power (the Anal phase), that it has value and a sense of worthiness (the Oedipal phase), and so on. If the person's needs are not sufficiently cared for, conflictual developmental results may be manifested in the different stages, such as lack of confidence in other people, dependency, sense of worthlessness, to name a few. Such manifestations are considered as a cause to psychopathology, crisis, and suffering later in life.

Accordingly, the overarching goal of the Dynamic therapy goal is to help the client solve conflicts in order to enable an adequate development of their personality. The Dynamic therapist aims at identifying the equilibrium point of conflict in the client's personality, and help them overcome obstacles in their journey to correct and heal their developmental process.

The premise is that there is a 'right' development of personality and obstacles that lead to suffering. It entails the assumption that an individual's attitude toward those obstacles can be corrected, hence enabling a more adequate development. Overall, on the basis of this premise, the Dynamic approach can be identified as corrective in essence. That said, it is important to note that there are branches and diversity in the various Dynamic therapeutic methods which may present other perspectives within this broad range.

The Cognitive Approach—The 'Self' as a System of Processing and Controlling the Stream of Consciousness

In the Cognitive approach, we find a shift from the concept of personality to a new central notion of the **Self**, that constitutes a command and control system over the human consciousness. To further understand this notion, we first examine the essence of consciousness according to this approach. Human consciousness is compiled of two central ingredients: stimulus and processing. The first can be seen as a wild and free 'stream' or 'sequence' of representations of the external reality, deriving from stimuli received by the human senses (i.e., visions, scents, voices, etc.). In other words, the stream of consciousness is seen as a river of ever-changing incentives, which changes from one moment to the next.

The 'river of consciousness' is ever streaming, ever changing, never calm. This is reflected in our dreams, which most often include a non-distinctive mix between our consciousness and a stream of unorganized representations of our reality—devoid of order, coherent organization, or meaning (See Fig. 4.1).

The second ingredient of consciousness is the processing and organizing of the various stimuli. This is followed by their representations in the

Fig. 4.1 The stream of consciousness

consciousness and arranging them into useful knowledge. This knowledge is used for the survival and everyday life of individuals in their reality and social environments. Several controlling and organizing centers are designed to capture images and representations that float freely in the stream of consciousness. This is followed by an operative framework of meaning for the person experiencing them, by comparing current stimuli to existing representations experienced in the past. From this, they project meanings and insights on the individual's future behavior, and thus manage their response to the different stimulating triggers.

In the human mind, there are different centers that process the ample information arriving from the external world. For example, the lingual center, among other functions, turns sounds and voices into a language, hence offering interpretation for them and infuses them with meaning for the listener. This center takes all the sounds captured by our ears at a given moment, and filters out those heard before, which indicate a certain meaning, like the word "hello". After recognizing the sounds related to the word 'hello' and attaching them to a certain meaning, it can examine which responses are available for a person who hears the word 'hello'.

That is how the lingual center manages hearing, and screens out the data that is relevant for adequate response. At the same time, it ignores less meaningful information, such as background noises. The philosopher Karl Wittgenstein (2009) compared the work of the lingual center to a fishing net that is thrown into the stream of consciousness, and fishes meaning out of it according to the way the individual's language is structured. This implies that each language would capture meanings differently, and create a different world of imagery in the mind of the individual.

In-between the different control and organization centers there exists a 'super-center'. This 'center' gathers all the information streaming from reality, through the images created in the consciousness that affects the individual. This center, known as the 'Self', is where we refer to ourselves as '**Me**', hence distinguishing ourselves from the external reality and view ourselves as unique and independent subjects.

As part of this center, individuals experience themselves as agents (or as an object of their awareness). They attribute to themselves an existence separated from the reality around them, and even from their own body. This center is in charge of attributing different qualities, emotions, thoughts and values to one's notions of identity and self-perception. This center is responsible for having an image of who we 'really are' in our mind, an image which includes certain values, perception of self-worth, self-image, social identity, sexual identity, professional identity, and so on (See Fig. 4.2).

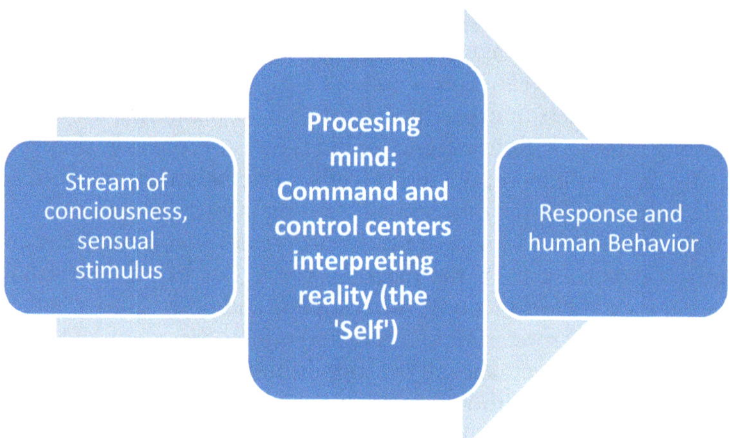

Fig. 4.2 The structure of consciousness and the role of the 'Self' in forming individual behavior

Cognitive psychology views the 'Self' as one of the central notions and main objects for research and intervention. This is based on the premise that understanding the 'Self' and its functions would explain to a great extent how individuals learn to comprehend and process the reality around them, and respond to it.

The more we learn about how the way this center operates, the more effectively we will be able to intervene, and to generate change in the behavior of individuals.

One of the main characteristics of the 'Self', according to the cognitive approach, can be compared to a modern computer, operating by predetermined cognitive patterns and scripts, which are forged by life experiences. In this sense, if an individual is raised in a village on the edge of a forest, knowing that whenever the bushes rustle, a tiger might emerge—he or she may develop a pattern that creates an association between rustling bushes and danger. In other words, cognitive psychology views human thinking patterns as habits based on past experience, while a change in life circumstances may nullify those patterns. Such patterns may range from adapted patterns adjusted to reality, to unadjusted patters that are inadequate for managing one's life.

For example, let's imagine that same person moves from the village in the forest to the big city, and hears rustling bushes while walking in the park. In this case, an alarm would be an inadequate response, because, obviously, there are no wild tigers in the city. According to this approach, psychological suffering is a result of a failure in thinking and interpreting reality. It stems from relying on behavioral patterns that were useful in the past (which is why they developed in the first place), yet turned destructive in a changed circumstances.

The objective of the therapeutic intervention is determined by this understanding—to 'correct' our thinking and behaving patterns and to adjust them to changing realities. The premise is that 'thinking habits and patterns' can be altered by training the mind. In other words, learning to reorganize and reinterpret the images and representations of reality, may lead to an adjusted and more efficient view and experience of the client's current situation. Again, the key word here is **correction**. It should be noted here, too, that while the classic approach is essentially corrective, current approaches present a wide range of focuses and perspectives for intervention. For example, the third wave cognitive therapies such as ACT have been greatly influenced by humanistic and existential models and are much less corrective in nature and much more related to understanding-collaboration models, as explained in the following section.

The Existential Approach—Dasein and the Sensual Experience at the Basis of Human Existence

Let's briefly revisit what cognitive psychology defined as the 'stream of consciousness', which represents our sensual experience of consciousness. As noted, the cognitive approach found it less interesting as a perspective for understanding human psychology. However, what is seen by the cognitive school as subordinate—is perceived by existentialists as central, or at least equally important to the processing and interpreting of the experience and its influence over behavior.

The sensual experience is embodied, in essence, in the **Dasein**, the condition of human consciousness before making existential choices that determine how one interprets their experience. Dasein is a completely subjective position devoid of any collective characteristics and interpretations that may be shared with others. Therefore, no one except for the experiencing individual has access to the 'lived experience' of another human being.

For example, a specific person's anger is recognizable according to certain signs typical of human anger in general. However, it still has a unique experience-related element of the person experiencing the anger—a subjective element that cannot be described and shared. In other words, Individual A's anger is always essentially different from individual B's anger—and so are their sorrows, joys, and so on.

In order to demonstrate the Dasein experience compared with the 'Self', we can use the right and the left brain functions as discussed previously. The 'right brain', which is subjective, emotional, and experience-based, is conflated with the rational, reasonable, and linear 'left brain', where control and processing centers interpret our experiences for us. The center of this organizational processing is known as the 'self' to which we attribute the very essence of our existence. It can be suggested that the 'left brain' operates similarly to the structure of consciousness according to cognitive psychology, namely stimulus-processing-response. At the same time, the 'right brain' works in a way that emphasizes the transformation from stimulus to response. As we have seen, there is sensual information ('lived experience and phenomenal data') necessary for the understanding the human consciousness within the activity of the right brain. Here we can find the experience we refer to as Dasein; the primary unique experience that 'colors' all our experiences of reality with personal subjective content. It could be described graphically as follows (See Fig. 4.3):

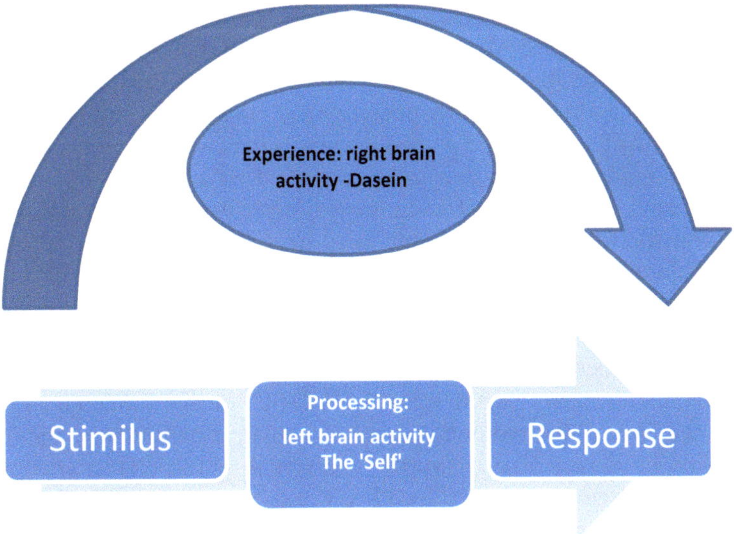

Fig. 4.3 The human consciousness structure between Dasein and 'Self'

From the above we may conclude that a therapeutic model based on the idea of right-brain sensational perception and consequent response **cannot** be essentially **corrective**. When we focus on the content of the Dasein's sensual experience we overrule our ability to interpret it as 'good' or 'bad' (left brain activity of interpretation). What remains, then?

The perception of the Dasein ('being here and now') is primary the sensational experience of reality, which is a holistic perception, and is always more than the sum of the different interpretations of the same reality. Viktor Frankl (Frankl, 1969, p. 9) demonstrates it with a tale of a neighbors' feud. Neighbor A claimed that neighbor B's cat had eaten his butter. He therefore demanded compensation. Neighbor B denied it, and a conflict erupted. They both turned to the village's wise elder for a resolution.

The elder asked two questions. The first was, "how much butter had the cat eaten?" to which neighbor A replied: 4.5 kg.

"And how much does the cat weigh?" asked the elder.

The cat was put on the scales and was found to weigh 4.5 kg.

"We found the butter!" stated the elder. "Now, where is the cat?"

In other words, reassembling the missing parts does not recreate the holistic living creature. We may be able to comprehend all the parts of a human entity (i.e., the self, the conscious and subconscious, or the cognitive schemes and patterns that operate it). However, we still struggle to grasp the living entity—the person—whose subjective experience is made of all those parts in a holistic and experiential way. In the same way, we cannot fully comprehend the client's experience just by understanding the symptom or the disease/suffering they describe. This would require a deeper understanding of their subjective experience, which is, according to this approach, the very objective of psychotherapy.

As the following figure illustrates, human consciousness is manifested as a synthesis between the brain's left ('analytical and rational') qualities and the brain's right ('experiential and holistic') qualities (See Fig. 4.4).

In the face of this synthetic model of human consciousness, the main intention in therapy is to accompany individuals in their direct encounter with their Dasein experience. In other words, we aim to rediscover their unique subjective experience in the world. The access to the Dasein

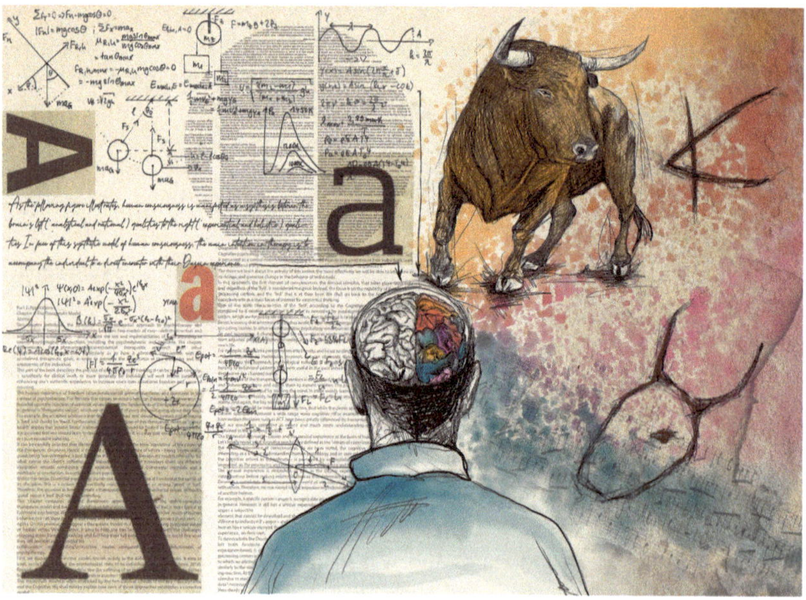

Fig. 4.4 The Human consciousness as a synthesis

may help the individual become more acquainted with other ways of living, and understand their choices thus far. As every person experiences reality distinctively and uniquely, the direct encounter with such experience has the power to reawaken the individual's sense of authenticity. With it, they can reclaim ownership and responsibility over their life.

The therapist in this approach, therefore, has no preference as to what is 'right' or 'wrong'. Their role is to direct the therapeutic process toward self-discovery and the insights it involves. The model for this kind of therapy is the accompanying model, or, in its more professional title, an understanding-collaboration model (e.g., Dubose, 2015). The above can be demonstrated by the following Jewish Hassidic tale attributed to Rabbi Nachman of Breslow (See Sadeh, 1982), according to which there was a young prince who went through a mental crisis and thought he was a turkey rather than a human being. He started behaving like a turkey, sat all day naked under the dining table at the palace's big hall, and pecked grains off the floor. He did not speak human language, only cackled in the language of turkeys.

The king and queen were very upset and worried. They invited the palace's doctor to take care of the young prince. The doctor did his best, to no avail. In the following week, a parade of doctors and wise men came to the palace from across the land. They tried everything: healing herbs, psychiatric medications, hypnosis, and exorcism—but nothing worked. When all hope was lost, and the prince still behaved like a turkey, a new wise man turned up one day, and asked the king and queen for a permission to let him try and help the prince.

When permission was granted, the wise man approached the prince, took his own clothes off, and sat with him under the table. Now, there were two big turkeys in the palace, and so they lived together like that for a while. After a week, when the turkeys established some connection, the wise man showed the prince that one can be a turkey in other ways as well. For example, one can stay a turkey but be 'a turkey who wears clothes' or 'a turkey that eats from a plate' and so on.

Through a long and slow process, the wise man helped the prince see the possibilities embedded in his basic experience of being a turkey, and expand the range of behaviors at his disposal beyond the basic script of 'sitting naked under the table and eating grains'. And so, the prince went back to behaving like a person, and eventually became a great wise monarch in his kingdom.

The Turkey story demonstrates the essence of the understanding-collaboration therapeutic model—each individual is a unique project, distinguishable from others, and no two people are the same (see Sartre, 2007). It can be said that every human is essentially 'a turkey', namely every person experiences reality differently to others (their 'Dasein' experience is different). However, an individual does not have to be a certain type of 'turkey'. One could be a 'turkey' in various different ways, including a turkey that sits at the table and eats using a fork and a knife.

The therapeutic approach, therefore, is accompanying the individual in their encounter with their Dasein—the preliminary human experience prior to a certain or specific interpretation or structure that may be applied to it. This may enable the freedom to reinterpret one's experience in a different and new way to the previously chosen ones. Such freedom provides the opportunity to see additional possibilities to live life more fully and meaningfully, even when facing challenging circumstances.

The difference between this model and the ones previously reviewed is the emphasis it places on freedom of choice.

Therefore, the most essential and important question for the Existential therapy model is how to bring a person into an encounter with their Dasein, direct experience of the here and now, in order to enable choice? And, how can we balance our existential concerns to enable a more authentic existence and awareness of our choices?

References

DuBose, T. (2015). Engaged understanding for lived meaning. *Journal of Contemporary Psychotherapy, 45*(1), 25–35.

Frankl, V. (1969). Reduction and nihilism. In A. Koestler & J. R. Smythies (Eds.), *Beyond reductionism*. Beacon Press.

Sadeh, P. (1982) [in Hebrew]. *Rabbi Nachman of Breslow: Stories, dreams, conversations*. Shokan.

Sartre, J. P. (2007). *Existentialism is a humanism* (C. Macomber, Trans.). Yale University Press.

Wittgenstein, L. (2009). *Philosophical investigations*. John Wiley & Sons.

CHAPTER 5

The Existential Approach in Practice—An Introduction

Abstract In this chapter, the three stages of the existential approach in practice are explained: being-for, being-alongside, and being-otherwise. Being-for involves the phenomenological measures implemented for the client to rediscover their taken-for-granted reality and for the practitioner to understand the client's subjective experience. Being-alongside involves the deconstruction of the client's subjective experience to its components, and understanding the universal concerns that are implied in their accounts and how they may influence their interpretation of reality. Being-otherwise involves searching together with the client for their unique way of being authentic as a "golden middle way" to embrace life's complexities, which allows getting in touch with life's givens.

Keywords Existential authenticity • Being-with psychotherapeutic model • Being-for stage • Being-alongside stage • Being-otherwise stage

As explained in previous chapters, humans deal differently with the universal concerns, and set up defenses (neurotic or denial-based), to help protect themselves from the existential anxiety that may accompany these concerns. This, in turn, leads to the construction of an inauthentic existence which is offers serenity and a sense of safety. However, when those defenses are too rigid, they might invoke distress.

J. Davidov, P. Russo-Netzer, *Existential Authenticity*,
https://doi.org/10.1007/978-3-031-07842-2_5

In such a situation of rigid defenses and subsequent distress, helping clients to rediscover their experience of being here-and-now, which may enable them to gain access to their inner freedom, and re-invoke their sense of responsibility over their life. These may contribute to enhance flexibility, while discovering new possibilities of how to experience any given moment.

To succeed in this goal, we must explore the individual's experience as they describe it, in order to better understand their subjective reality and how they may experience existential anxiety. More specifically, we aim at exploring the different aspects of existential anxiety as manifested in the clients' subjective experience, to better understand which ones the individual essentially finds harder to accept (is it the concern of death, isolation, freedom, or meaninglessness?).

Once we establish insights regarding the universal concerns as they play out in the individual's account for their lifeworld, we can help the client increase his or her authentic existence. This is achieved by offering clients who express rigid neurotic-based defenses—helpful tools to regulate excessive anxiety, and to clients who express rigid denial-based defenses—offering helpful tools to regulate depression and alienation. In either case, the therapist aspires to introduce clients to their authentic experience of reality as a "golden middle way", which involves the right dose of existential anxiety, an amount they can tolerate and contain without being pushed to activate their inauthentic defenses.

The Dasein Approach and Existential Authenticity

The first focus of the therapeutic process is in understanding the client's subjective experience of their distress. The premise here is that any human account is constructed from both components of consciousness, the rational and organizing aspect as well as the sensory and experiential aspect. As such, the first step is to learn to separate the two while listening to the client's given account. Whether the clients discuss their professional work, friendships, romantic relationship, family interaction, hobbies or culinary preferences, their accounts are always constructed from both elements. The therapists' primary task at this stage is to learn to differentiate the two elements so that they could focus on the subjective experience in the following stages.

The second step that follows is the identification of the universal concerns that are embedded in the client's lived experience. This involves actively searching for certain **meaning clues** which characterize each concern in the client's narrative and using these 'clues' to assess the dominant universal concern which is implicated in the current account of the client's distress.

Finally, focusing on a specific concern that influences the narrative, and learning how it may affect the client's lived experience (i.e., denial or neurosis)—enable the therapist to move on to the last part of therapy. In this final stage, we aim at 'balancing the equation' in order to bring the clients toward a closer encounter with their authentic moderated experience of existential anxiety. This may be achieved by helping them experience the right dose of anxiety they can contain, which yields a rediscover of possibilities for change. At this point we can use different tools from various practices (i.e., cognitive, dynamic and so on), in order to open up the new choices that may be relevant and applicable to the client's life.

Wong (2010) suggests that in doing this, each universal concern can be transformed into a virtue which enables empowered authentic life as illustrated below:

From death concern to **accepting** the finality of life and **coming to terms** with the constant changing nature of life.

From freedom concern to **taking responsibility** for one's own choices and constructing a sense of integrity.

From isolation concern to the ability of **being in intimate relationship with others** and a chance of love.

From meaninglessness concern to **active participation** in life and finding meaning in the world.

We shall discuss each of those virtues of authentic existence when we look deeper into each of the existential concerns separately. At this point, we present the general work plan of the therapeutic approach that is focused on 'existential authenticity'.

The intervention plan of the 'existential authenticity' approach is comprised of three stages (Dubose, 2015):

1. Being for—The goal at this stage is to use phenomenological tools of active listening to the client's narrative, in order to comprehend

their lived experience in the context in which it occurred: work; personal relationship; parenthood and so on. The phenomenological discourse aims to create a facilitating space in which the client rediscovers their 'taken for granted'. With that, they can learn more about the premises, patterns or themes that organize their subjective experience. This stage is necessary to create the foundation for the client to understand their experience of existential anxiety and the defenses they may operate in order to avoid it. Meanwhile, the therapist gets closer to the client's experience, realizing 'what it is like' to be the client. This, in turn, establishes the therapeutic partnership and the ability to collaborate and accompany the client in encountering their subjective lifeworld. Additionally, the therapist learns to identify patterns in the client's account of their lifeworld relating to the four existential modes of subjective experience of temporality, embodiment, relationality, or spatiality. As we shall see, these existentials are related to the different types of universal concerns (i.e., death, freedom, etc.); hence, they are used as clues and guidelines that may pave the way to the second stage of therapy.

2. Being alongside—At this stage, the goal is to 'capture' the authentic experience of the client and to understand how he or she finds meaning in their life. This is done by attempting to identify the dominant universal concerns that are implied in the client's everyday life account, and the manner in which they may affect the client's lifeworld (subjective experience). For example, we may ask whether the client deals with her Isolation concern neurotically or through denial?
3. Being otherwise—At this stage, the client learns to moderate their concerns in order to achieve a more authentic experience that may lead to a profound change in their life. The goal here is to offer the client possible routes, pathways and tools that may open new possibilities for interpreting their experience and that may available to them when existential anxiety is at bay. Such possibilities reestablish situational freedom and provide the client with the opportunity to regain responsibility and enhance a sense of control and meaning in life.

In the next chapters, we take a closer look at each of these stages of therapy separately, while introducing applicable tools and techniques that can be used at any stage to promote the process of intervention. We also present an integrated map of existential authenticity which aim to bridge one's and the universal concerns. This map may be helpful for therapists in identifying existential concerns in the client's accounts and in planning possible directions for intervention that would increase their levels of authenticity.

References

DuBose, T. (2015). Engaged understanding for lived meaning. *Journal of Contemporary Psychotherapy, 45*(1), 25–35.

Wong, P. T. P. (2010). What is existential positive psychology? *International Journal of Existential Psychology & Psychotherapy, 3*(1), 1–10.

CHAPTER 6

Being-for the Client and the Phenomenology of the Subjective Experience

Abstract This chapter explores in depth the first step of this therapy, which aims to achieve the two complementary goals of helping the client rediscover their taken-for-granted reality and identify major themes that cause them distress and enabling the practitioner to better understand what it is like to be "in the client's skin" through the exploration of the client's lifeworld existentials. It provides a preliminary introduction to the various tools for exploring the client's lived experience—bracketing, horizontalization and descriptive clarification—that are elaborated in subsequent chapters. It also introduces the use of descriptive, structural, and prompting/stimulating questions to better capture the client's lived experience.

Keywords Rediscover the taken-for-granted • Bracketing • Horizontalization • Descriptive clarification • Descriptive questions • Structural • Prompting/stimulating questions • 'What is it like to be the client' • The four lifeworld existentials in practice

The main element of the first stage of intervention is based on active listening. The therapist bears in mind that each client is a different and unique "project" and that their story should be heard in the "cleanest" way possible. The client should be heard while neutralizing or framing the therapist's prejudices and assumptions which might mislead the therapist

J. Davidov, P. Russo-Netzer, *Existential Authenticity*,
https://doi.org/10.1007/978-3-031-07842-2_6

as to how the client constructs their lifeworld's experience. Additionally, the therapist in listening to the client's story, should separate the rational and organized part of the story from the sensual and emotional part of the story in order to be able to focus on the subjective experience. In other words, a technique that can focus on listening to the lived experience "from the bottom up" is required. This technique is more important than the client's interpretation of what had happened to them "from the top down" as it aims to capture the client's lifeworld as they experienced it.

As previously discussed (see Chap. 2), the relevant technique for this aim was developed in the early twentieth century. It was known as "phenomenology"—the theory of a phenomenon as it is presented and experienced by the human consciousness.

As we saw in Chap. 2, phenomenology provides valuable tools for existential thinking. It contributes significantly to the understanding of the individual's unique point of view regarding the reality in which they operate, with minimal preemptive interpretation. Thus it is the premise of every existential therapy.

There are two therapeutic goals in using phenomenology as a therapeutic method. One relates to the client and the other to the therapist. We shall examine each of them separately.

Client-Focused Goal: To Rediscover What Was Taken for Granted

The first goal of the therapist using phenomenology as a therapeutic method is to rediscover the hidden themes, namely the personal issues characterizing the client, that are at the heart of all of the client's experiences. The phenomenological premise is that every individual has a subjective experience that colors their whole life's narrative. In addition, it can be assumed that this experience can be conceptualized by the client into the main issues that occupy them at a certain time. For example, a pregnant woman would suddenly notice all the pregnant women around her, a person anxious about contracting a viral disease (e.g., COVID-19), would take note of "dangerous" and "safe" areas and an individual with an interest in fashion would notice what others are wearing. However, these are only superficial examples. Every person has deep themes that guide their outlook and the way they observe the world. Those themes are this person's "taken-for-granted" reality. They reflect things that preoccupy them continuously, and that even they cannot conceptualize, because they are so close to their heart.

Such themes are also known in the scientific literature as "provinces of meaning" (Schutz & Luckmann, 1973) or islands containing significant ingredients for the individual experiencing them, distinguishable from the general reality around them. The purpose of the phenomenological quest is to distinguish between the individual and their personal taken-for-granted issues—those islands of meaning in their consciousness. The goal is for the client to be able to view these issues from a certain distance and not out of a notion that they embody "who they are". This constitutes a separation of the individual from their sense of self. It helps them to look at it as there being a certain distance between the constituting and subjective experience of reality.

At this stage, the work is inductive, namely, investigating the clients' experiences that are described in detail in the client's own words. It aims toward a joint discovery of the meaningful themes that organize the subjective experience of the client's lifeworld reality.

At the heart of inductive thinking is active and curious listening, for which there are a few different techniques. In this book, we describe three of the main ones (e.g. Dubose, 2015), which also constitute three phases of the conversation with the client:

- Bracketing
- Horizontalization
- Descriptive clarification

The first and most important phase, Bracketing, means suspending judgment over a certain narrative and deliberately avoiding an external analysis of the experience. Take, for example, the experience of COVID-19 and the lockdown, which was so different from our previous way of living. If we ask an individual about their lockdown experience we might hear that it was "very hard" for them.

From a human perspective, we can generally understand what people mean by this response. However, from a phenomenological point of view we must remember that any experience is subjective, and that no one has direct access to another person's experience.

In other words, the hardship experienced by one person in lockdown is unique to this individual. The therapist must remember this and constantly remind themself that language is a collection of agreed upon sounds that indicate intention. However, it does not contain the subjective experience implied by this intention. That is to say, the therapist must apply the "tower of Babylon" notion. Even if the therapist seems to understand the client's words, they must question the meaning that those words point to.

The therapist must constantly wonder: What do the words mean? What does hardship mean for this specific client? The process of bracketing aims at the therapist. It should help silence the therapist's inner interpretative voices to enable them to gain descriptive knowledge of the client's subjective (sensual or emotional) experience without attempting to interpret it.

Obviously, it is not easy to listen to the client phenomenologically in a way that constantly questions everything the client says, especially all that has to do with emotional and sensual experiences. To activate the bracketing technique, the therapist who encounters a subjective emotion, sensation, or subjective experience begins to wonder out loud about its nature. Those questions originate from a position known as "educated naiveté" constantly and deliberately questioning their knowledge regarding the subjective experience of the client speaking to them.

The purpose of those questions is to push the client into exploring their own subjective experience and question their own taken-for-granted life-world reality. Thus, the therapist prompts the client to go on a journey of self-exploration and to ask questions about the premises constructing their subjective world.

James Spradley (1979) suggested three types of questions that can help ignite this process of exploration. He raised them in the context of ethnographic research, but we shall use his outline here for the purpose of phenomenological exploration: descriptive questions, structural questions, and prompting/stimulating questions—designed to uncover contradictions and similarities. Each of these question types is suitable for a different phase of the phenomenological conversation.

The descriptive questions call for a detailed description of the sensual or emotional phenomenon the client speaks of. They are particularly suitable for the phase in which the therapist seeks a detailed picture of the subjective experience from the 'educated naiveté' position, while **bracketing** the therapist's knowledge about the client's subjective experience.

Going back to the previous example, when a therapist hears that a client experienced hardship during lockdown, the therapist should ask questions aiming for as rich a description of the experience as possible:

1. Grand tour questions. These are to be used when we ask, in a comprehensive, inviting, and open way, for the client to describe an issue they mentioned. The goal is to understand the context in which the event noted by the client took place, in the way they choose to mention it. It usually consists of extensive use of the "what" question. **What** are the most meaningful issues for a person in a given context? For example, "tell me what was meaningful for you about lockdown and how was your life influenced by it." This inquiry would yield an answer that includes reference to the client's provinces of meaning (meaningful subjective issues) that were influenced by lockdown.
2. Mini-tour questions. These questions seek more details about one of those provinces of meaning that was raised in response to the grand tour question. For example, "You said your work was compromised; could you tell me more about your work?"
3. Example questions. These reference an event or a certain aspect mentioned by the client and request an example. For instance, "You said you are a team leader. Could you give me an example of what you do in your role?"
4. Experience questions. These are questions that prompt the client to focus on a certain feeling in their experience. For example, "Now, that I understand the framework in which you work a bit better, let's get to what you said earlier about your work being compromised. Could you now explain to me more clearly how exactly it was compromised?"

The above are examples of questions for investigating in depth an individual's subjective experience. At the same time, they seek a detailed description of the meaningful subjective issues raised by the clients. The more detailed the description is, the more experience-based details it would include. In other words, at the heart of the detailed description is a connection to the subjective experience, and less analytical interpretation. Therefore, more than anything, it is important to ask for as many details as possible about senses and emotions relating to the experience.

While striving for detail-rich descriptions (the first stage), the therapist also aims to understand the client's provinces of meaning. In particular, the therapist is interested in what the experience holds and symbolizes for the client. For example, a client describing in detail how their work was compromised by the lockdown implies their workplace has a deep meaning for them. The therapist needs to figure out what exactly that meaning is for their client.

The second phase, also known as Horizontalization, is the stage in which the therapist asks questions about the meaning that is implied in the client's experience. More specifically, it aims to comprehend the meaning of the experience out of the context in which it was told and in relation to the specific terms used by the client.

The second phase, also known as Horizontalization, is the stage in which the therapist asks questions about the meaning that is implied in the client's experience. More specifically, it aims to comprehend the meaning of the experience out of the context in which it was told and in relation to the specific terms used by the client.

The therapeutic conversation at this stage focuses on an attempt to understand, together with the client, what the experience means for them, by exploring the contextual frame in which this meaning is constructed. Here, the therapist would keep asking questions out of the position of educated naiveté. But this time the therapist would seek central terms, or "molecular words". Those terms bear weight and meaning, and they influence the client's way of thinking. The questions used in this stage can expose the main terms and context vital for understanding the experience. For example, the meaning of the client's workplace can be examined through questions about the setting and the client's occupational history. It can also be explored by looking into the client's professional identity and its development throughout the years and their expectations from the job, from themselves, and so on.

For this purpose, Spradley (1979) offers structural questions that examine how individuals organize their subjective knowledge about an experience, and fill it with meaning. Such questions include:

1. Why questions. First and foremost, asking the "why question" to better understand **why** the mentioned issues are so meaningful for the client. The most important issue here is to capture the context and frame of reference in which those issues are significant for the client. Following the above example, a general type of structural question about the workplace may be, "You said that your work is very meaningful for you. In order to understand why your work is so meaningful and in what way, I would like to further understand your conceptualization of the concept of 'work' and how you experience it. Please try to explain to me why and in what way your work has become so meaningful for you."
2. Term clarification questions. These ask the client to clarify terms that they take for granted, such as: "What does success mean for you?", or "Tell me about your aspirations and aims regarding your work."

3. Meaning clarification questions. These are questions relating to the intention behind certain behavior or the use of certain terms. For example, "What do you mean by being assertive?"
4. Position questions. These prompt the client to express an opinion about a certain topic that came up in conversation. For example, "What do you think about your boss?" or "What do you feel about your role and position at your workplace?"

Example 6.1
Dana, a 45-year-old woman, shared her experience of giving a presentation to a large audience at a conference. In order to better understand why this presentation was significant for her, structural questions were used to clarify the experience. The questions aimed to capture the contextual frame that explained the significance of the experience. This context could range from a performance anxiety rooted in an unfortunate experience back in puberty, to a need for perfectionism, or anything else. As such, structural questions are used to identify the core issues that may underlie a significant experience.

The third and last phase of the phenomenological conversation is Descriptive Clarification. It aims to examine the connections between different meaningful issues reviewed in previous stages, for example, the connection between work-related issues and other provinces of meaning that came up in conversation, such as family, hobbies, education, or sports. Each of those areas of life has meaning for the client, as they have chosen to discuss them. The premise is that there is a connection between all meaning areas that the client is asked to clarify. The final aim is to try and decipher the subjective map of the client that illustrates the relationships between the numerous and unique provinces of meaning that were identified in previous stages. In this sense, 'descriptive clarification' refers to an attempt to gain an in-depth 'bottom-up' understanding of what the client means, rather than relying on 'top-down' interpretation from previous knowledge.

The main technique is using prompting/stimulating questions in order to challenge the client to seek connections among the meaning areas they mentioned. The therapist aims to help the client figure out the inner map that guides their life and defines what is "hard", "interesting", "challenging", "frightening" etc. Prompting/stimulating questions mostly examine the boundaries and values of an individual, as manifested in different areas in their life. For that purpose, we suggest the following questions:

1. The "how" questions. First and foremost is asking **"how** one implements the meaning discussed in earlier phases to different provinces of meaning in their life that are important to them?"
2. Questions regarding the connection between meaning areas. For example: "You have just spoken at length about your workplace and your professional identity. You clarified they are very important meaning-areas for you. However, you also mentioned your family as a meaning-area earlier. How are those areas connected for you, and how do they influence each other and your life in general?"
3. Contrast questions. These are used when clients contradict themselves in a way that requires clarifications. For example, "You said your family is the most important thing in your life, but now you said professional development was the most important thing in your life. How do you balance the tension between those two meaningful areas in your life?"
4. Questions of comparison and conflict. These are used when we want to confront the client with issues that came up while discussing other experiences. For example, "You said your family provides you with self-worth. Now you have added that work also contributes to your self-worth, but in a different way. Could you specify how is the self-worth you derive from your family similar to the self-value that comes from your work? How are they different?"

Example 6.2
Following up on the structural questions asked, Dana shared that presenting at a conference was significant for her because of her childhood experience and specifically due to her experience of being shy, avoiding social interactions as much as possible. After discussing her shyness, the descriptive clarification stage aimed to understand how this concern influenced other provinces of meaning in Dana's life such as her parenthood, her relationship with her spouse, and other meaningful areas in her life. Such prompting/stimulating questions allow for exploration of how "being shy" has manifested along different lifeworld areas and how it influenced her life as a whole.

In sum, we presented three types of questions: descriptive (in particular what questions), structural (in particular why questions) and prompting/stimulating (in particular how questions). Using them puts the phenomenological question-asking technique into practice. Additionally, they can get us closer to capturing the client's meaningful issues that are embedded in the experience they chose to share in therapy. Any subjective experience can be explored this way, including joy, anger, depression, romantic feelings, and so on.

When the process is implemented skillfully, clients feel that they rediscover their taken-for-granted lived experience. Thus, they acquire a new level of consciousness regarding their ways of thinking and of giving meaning to their experiences.

Going back to the previous example of the lockdown experience during the COVID-19 pandemic, the client would enhance their awareness as to the way in which they experienced hardship. They would find out what is unique about the way they experienced it and what their experience was constructed of. Generally, they would discover how this hardship relates to the wider context of their life.

In other words, they would rediscover how they produce feelings of hardship and what it is made of for them. This reflexive observation will lead us to the next stage of the therapeutic process which includes a direct exposure to the universal concerns that are implied in their lifeworld. But first, there is another important phenomenological area to cover, and that is the therapist's own understanding of the client's subjective experience—the therapist's interpretative view of the client's lifeworld.

Therapist-Focused Goal: What Is It Like to Be the Client?

So far, we have seen how the therapist can challenge the client into gaining insight about their subjective experience and how it influences their worldview. Beyond the questions that help the client to be aware of their 'taken for-granted' issues, the therapist needs to understand the client's experience as much as possible as if they were the client themselves. For this purpose, the therapist can use secondary type of questions that will assist them to explore the client's modes of experience to make them more accessible for bottom-up interpretation.

In the first part of the book we asserted that every experience is constructed out of the four lifeworld existential modes of temporality, embodiment, relationality and spatiality (see the discussion of hermeneutic phenomenology in Chap. 2). This knowledge can be used as an interpretive tool to explore the existential mode that is salient in the client's accounts of their lifeworld.

In this book, we offer a two-step approach to capture the client's mode of experience. The first step is utilizing Gendlin's technique of "Focusing" to connect the client to their felt-sense of the issue discussed (see Gendlin, 1982). Felt sense is the physiological aspect of any given human experience. In this regard, any thought a person might have, any action they take, or any image they contemplate has an accompanying unique felt sense that each person can connect to. Gendlin suggests that any situation or human being we encounter, every period in life has its own felt-sense. He maintains that this feeling is the expression of the concentrated knowledge a person holds of a phenomenon in a given context. If, for example, a client has discussed their work as a meaningful area in their life, the therapist may ask them to focus on the felt sense of this meaningful area and how it feels in their body.

The second step is to explore the identified felt-sense as it manifests along the four lifeworld existentials: temporality, embodiment, relationality and spatiality.

Temporality

Questions regarding temporality examine the flowing of time in the accounts shared by the client. The focus is on checking to what extent temporality is experienced as flowing and focused on the "now" (flowing relates to a balanced connection between acting and thinking, when the individual is focused on the action and does not feel the passing time, the Dasein experience). Those questions also explore to what extent temporality is experienced as slow-paced (having a past orientation, sinking into thinking) or, alternatively, occupied with the next moment and always rushing away (future orientation, focused on action).

After a mutual discussion, we can ask the client to pick a position on the range displayed in Table 6.1, which illustrates the experience spectrum of temporality for a client, as introduced in the first part of this book (Table 6.1).

An Exercise Demonstrating Temporality

Think about your life today. Focus on a certain meaning-area (career, relationship, family, and so on). Consider your temporality (or rhythm) as experienced in that context.

- To what extent do you feel stuck in the past, prefer to ponder and be deep in thought, or, in contrast, are always in a hurry, occupied with the "next thing" on your life's sequence, always in action?
- To what extent do you feel "flowing", with thought and action connected to each other, unaware of the passing time?

Table 6.1 Conscious experience of temporality

Split awareness focused on 'there isn't'	Being-here Dasein	Split awareness focused on 'there is'
'There is no time'	**'Being now'**	**'There is time'**
Fast pace, being in action	Being in the moment, focused, unity of thought and action	Slow pace, being introspective

The rhythm that clients determine for themselves is important for future therapeutic work. The modes of subjective experience and the extent of deviation from the Dasein (marked at the center of the range) provide significant data about the client's lifeworld. They imply a salient universal concern, as we shall see in the next chapter.

We note that clients often find it hard to point out which side away from the flowing center they are disposed toward. Still, it is important to figure out how remote or close they feel to a balancing sense of Dasein in the relevant context. The distance and the extent of the deviation are a significant indication for next stages of therapeutic work.

Embodiment

Questions regarding embodiment examine how individuals experience in their felt bodies and sense of self the event they are discussing. The focus here is on the sense of capability or self-value that a person feels in a certain context. In other words, to what extent do they feel a balancing

An exercise demonstrating working with embodiment:
Think again about different contexts in your life's space (work, home, your parents' home, etc).

- Consider the physical sensations each context invokes in you. To what extent do you feel that you are flexible and capable of changing (forming)?
- To what extent do you feel diminished or restrained? Alternatively, to what extent do you feel assertive, empowered, leading, with a clear and high-presence impact on your surroundings?

Table 6.2 Conscious experience of embodiment

Split consciousness, focused on 'there isn't'	Being-here Dasein	Split consciousness, focused on 'there is'
'There is no self'	**Being present, ever evolving, forming**	**'There is a self'**
Low-impact presence		high-impact presence

experience of being "present" in a situation (the Dasein experience)? Alternatively, to what extent do they feel a high-impact presence in the relevant context (an experience of "there is a clear and dominant sense of self")? Or to what extent do they feel low-impact presence, and sense that there is no sense of self".

After a mutual discussion of this matter we may ask the client to pick a position and demonstrate the experience of embodiment for them in relation to the context they picked (see Table 6.2).

Relationality

Questions regarding relationality examine how an individual experiences their significant others in their life. What feelings get invoked in clients in the presence of others? Here, the focus is on how much does an individual feel that they belong and are a part of the context they are discussing (the balancing experience of 'being together', or Dasein)? Alternatively, to what extent do they feel merged ('there is clear relationships to the

An exercise demonstrating working with relationality:
Consider significant people in your life in different contexts (work, home, etc.)

- What do they symbolize for you? To what extent do you feel partnership with those people?
- To what extent do you feel separated and isolated from others?
- To what extent do you feel merged and inseparable?

Table 6.3 Conscious experience of relationality

Split consciousness, focused on 'there isn't' **'There are no others'** There is only isolation, 'lone wolf' position, being different	Being-here Dasein **'Being together'** Connection, partnership between equals	Split consciousness, focused on 'there is' **'There is clear sense of others'** Complete merging, a team player' position

others') or separated and isolated in the context of a relationship ('there are no others').

After a mutual discussion of this matter, we may ask the client to pick a position, demonstrating the experience of relationality for them (Table 6.3).

Spatiality

Finally, we examine the spatial experience of the client in the various contexts they discuss. To what extent do they feel that the space they occupy in different provinces of meaning in their life can be influenced and changed (namely, are they dynamic)? Alternatively, to what extent do they feel stuck in boundaries that are too rigid for them (a "clear space" experience)? Or in different settings, to what extent do they feel the boundaries to be too loose (a "no clear space" experience)?

Any place that is experienced as significant for the individual is a trigger for a conversation about what is essential for them about that space (figure) and what is less important (background). Particularly, what does this place (or context) enable the individual to express, and what does it prevent. In other words, to what extent does the place or realm enable playfulness and flexibility and open up opportunities to influence its surroundings (the balancing position, "being-here", or Dasein)? In different cases, to what extent does it narrow down and diminish options? Or, is it a too chaotic and undefined spatiality that might cause bewilderment and sense of "being lost"?

An exercise demonstrating working with spatiality.
Think about significant places in your life (work, home, nature, etc.). Consider what is essential for you about those places (figure) and what is less important (background).

- To what extent do you experience the place as having clear and rigid rules on the one hand, or being alienated, wanton, and chaotic, on the other hand?
- How much does the place allow you to examine possibilities while maintaining a sense of safety? Or to what extent does it let you play with different options and influence it?

After a mutual discussion of this matter, we may ask the client to pick a position, demonstrating the range of spatiality for them in relation to the context they picked (see Table 6.4).

Here, too, the client's position regarding the spatial range and the way it relates to the center point of Dasein contains important information about the client's experience. It will contribute to subsequent stages of the therapeutic process, as we shall see later.

The map displayed in Table 6.5 can be introduced and filled in by the client and therapist together—at the end of the exploration of the existential modes of experience (Table 6.5).

Table 6.4 Conscious experience of spatiality

Split consciousness focused on 'there isn't'	Being here Dasein	Split consciousness focused on 'there is
'There is no clear space' the need for an open ended space, flexible rules in order to thrive	**A dynamic sense of ability to influence the space**	**'There is a clear space'** Structured areas, clear rules and order are needed to thrive

Table 6.5 The map of subjective experience—'what is it like to be the client'

Split consciousness focused on 'there isn't'	Being-here Dasein	Split consciousness focused on 'there is'
'There is no time' fast rhythm	**Now**	'There is time' slow rhythm
Low impact presence'	**Present**	'High impact presence'
There is no other/ lone wolf	**Together**	There is another/ team player
'There are borders/ structured space	**Here**	'There are no borders/ open space'

This map offers an opportunity to learn about the subjective experience of the client from a bottom-up position, as it helps to explore how it is organized along the four existential modes of subjective experience.

The goal is to get the individual to recognize and mark for themselves the existential modes of experience that are less balanced. As we shall see in the next chapter, the various modes of experience include meaningful hints, indicating different universal concerns. It may help focus them on a relevant salient universal concern that is implied in their account. Therefore, they provide important information for the subsequent intervention stage of "being with" the clients.

References

DuBose, T. (2015). Engaged understanding for lived meaning. *Journal of Contemporary Psychotherapy, 45*(1), 25–35.

Gendlin, E. T. (1982). Focusing. Bantam.

Schutz, A., & Luckmann, T. (1973). *The structures of the life world* (Vol. 1). Northwestern University Press.

Spradley, P. J. (1979). *The ethnographic interview*. Holt.

CHAPTER 7

The Being-Alongside Stage and the Client's Universal Concerns

Abstract This chapter offers a heuristic model of the phenomenological structure of existential anxiety to help therapists identify salient features of the concept in their clients' subjective experiences, even when those are implicit in their accounts. The theoretical model is based on a broad, in-depth study of transformative life experiences, which offers a systematic phenomenological approach to explore existential anxiety. The model allows therapists and clients to identify implicit universal concerns that organize and frame the client's subjective experience and to better understand how those concerns shape their perceived reality and cause dysfunctional defense mechanisms that might cause pain and distress.

Keywords The association between lifeworld mode of experience and the universal concerns • Transformative life experiences • Existential anxiety • Universal concerns • Lifeworld existentials

At this stage, the therapist and the client are ready to find out what the narrative means for the client, and particularly—which universal concern "manages" them. This is the concern around which their defenses system (neurotic or denial-based) aligns. It is the core of that system that causes suffering and distress and may undermine their mental health. The premise is that when distress is accounted-for, there is one salient aspect of existential anxiety that can be identified in the form of one of the universal

J. Davidov, P. Russo-Netzer, *Existential Authenticity*, https://doi.org/10.1007/978-3-031-07842-2_7

concerns. It affects and colors the client's subjective lifeworld experience with specific emotions and sensations (Davidov & Russo-Netzer, 2021). In other words, in every context of the client's life, and in any account they present to the therapist—a salient universal concern is presented, though it is important to note that in different contexts different concerns may apply. The therapist must be sensitive and attentive enough to the client's account in order to identify the concern presented in a given context.

Understanding the dominant universal concern in a therapy session would also point at the authentic experience of the client. As noted earlier, four universal concerns exist: death, freedom, isolation and meaninglessness. From those concerns, four paths lead to authenticity. When we "capture" the client's universal concern, no matter which path we take, we can harness it to balance the anxiety and to help the client achieve a more authentic way of being in the world.

In some cases, for example, the therapist and the client identify the centrality of the concern of death. Around it, the client has developed obsessive defenses of endless activity. In such a case, the therapeutic path would focus on narrowing down the client's anxiety. This, in turn, would enable them to experience a more authentic experience of accepting finality and coming to terms with the constant changing of being. Identifying the dominant concern and capturing the authentic experience are central foci for this stage in the intervention process.

However, in many cases the universal concern is not articulated in a clear manner and is only implied in the client's account of their distress. Most clients do not describe their anxiety in terms like "the concern of death", or "the concern of freedom", and so on. Those are terms that prevail within existential thinking, but they are not organic in spoken language. Therefore, a "bridge" is required to associate the client's experience as they live it, to the universal concern characterizing their accounts regarding their subjective lifeworld.

It is important to note that this is the central phase in all of the various branches of existential therapy. Most existing literature points out the importance of dynamic and meaningful exploration deep into the universal concerns. This exploration aims to reach meaningful insight and prompt a change in the client's life.

Different therapeutic approaches focus on different concern channels, such as the concern of death (Terror Management Theory; TMT), isolation (gestalt etc.), and meaning-seeking (logotherapy and so on). The purpose of this book is to suggest, based on extensive research by the authors (Davidov & Russo-Netzer, 2021), a more dynamic bridge between an individual's experiences, as accounted for in natural language, and the universal concerns that are implied in the narratives. Such a bridge, or a map, of how to explore a subjective experience can lead to insights crucial for the next and final stage of intervention of moderating anxiety into a more authentic way of life.

A Bridge Between the Modes of Lifeworld Experience and Existential Concerns

The extensive study we conducted included 200 in-depth interviews. We found that when an interviewee accounts for a Transformative Life Experiences (TLE)—an event that causes significant change in their life or perceived reality—they in fact **account for an authentic moment**. In that moment, a realization awakens. In other words, they understand that their life so far was based on a certain interpretation of their circumstances.

This means that a TLE is an authentic encounter with the awareness of Dasein. In its course, an individual discovers there are other ways to experience their life. Consequently, a situational freedom is established, enabling them to choose to live differently.

Descriptions of TLEs are actually reports of an authentic subjective experience. During such moments, core beliefs, identities and a rigid self-perception momentarily fall away, and expose the universal concerns at their core (death, freedom, isolation, or meaninglessness). Active listening to a TLE is a particularly useful tool for understanding how to lead a change in the client's way of being in the world. The authentic experience that is exposed there can be harnessed and used in any other context in the client's life that involves suffering or distress.

More specifically, the study establishes a heuristic theoretical relationship between the four universal concerns of death, freedom, isolation, and meaninglessness to the phenomenological modes of experience (temporality, embodiment, relationality and spatiality). Such interplay may provide a systematic approach to one's subjective experience, in order to identify a dominant universal concern in a given context. Table 7.1 presents the possible association between each lifeworld mode of experience and the related existential concern.

Table 7.1 The association between lifeworld mode of experience and the universal concerns

Existential mode of Experience	*Universal Concern*	*Existential Anxiety*
Temporality	Concern of Death	Fear of Finality and failure
Embodiment	Concern of Freedom	Fear of Guilt
Relationality	Concern of Isolation	Fear of Exposure and shame
Spatiality	Concern of Meaninglessness	Fear of Uncertainty

This table may be used to deepen the conversation with the client. It enables the therapist to explore the lived experience to identify the universal concern at the core of the account under scrutiny. It is, in fact, the purpose of this stage of therapy, to "be with" the client—to explore their existential concerns together and to figure out how they influence their experience.

We shall address practical intervention and the manner of utilizing the insights arising from the study for the therapeutic encounter and for personal growth in the next and final chapter. But, first, we look into examples from the study that demonstrate the emerging association between the dominant modes of lifeworld experience and universal concerns.

For each mode of experience, we present two accounts of TLEs. One account demonstrates a TLE that marks a shift from a neurotic realm of defense ("there is anxiety") to a more authentic way of being in the world. The other points at a shift from a denial-based defense ("there is no anxiety") to a more authentic stance.

Examples of TLEs related to the dominant experience mode of temporality, and the concern of death:

The following examples are events reported in the study, that are related to the dominant experience mode of temporality. They exemplify the association with the concern of death accompanying this mode of experience.

The first example reveals an experience of temporality that shifts from a future facing orientation and an accelerated pace of life, to a sense of slowing pace and more 'authentic' flow of time. The interviewee was a 27-year-old female from a religious conservative background. She went through a TLE when her sister was injured in a serious car accident nine years prior to the interview.

Before the TLE, the interviewee practiced religious rites and duties such as observing the sanctity of Shabbat and holidays, keeping kosher, and other Jewish practices. She reported that she always lived while getting ready for the next moment: the next Shabbat meal, the next holiday feast, and so on. She generally lived with a clear future-facing orientation and a sense of the fast and ever-changing pace of life. In other words, the interviewee lived her life in constant activity, always gearing up for the next moment.

But one Friday, just as Shabbat was approaching, the grave news arrived: her sister had been injured in a serious car accident. The news brought chaos into the family's life that weekend, especially into the life of the interviewee. Her sister was very dear to her, and she urgently needed to get to the hospital, be next to her, and hold her hand. It was the first time that she broke the rules of observing Shabbat. But, furthermore, she suddenly realized that the present, the current moment, was all that mattered, and that the next moment might never come, never occur.

Those thoughts brought her to the conclusion that the life she had led so far, constantly getting ready for the next moment, was wrong—that it gave her a false sense of security, a delusion that "all will be fine". She realized that those were defense mechanisms shielding her from the precariousness of life and its temporary nature. She concluded that her previous life was a constant attempt to protect herself from the fear of death that she felt lurked at every moment, everywhere.

Following the accident and her realizations, the interviewee changed her lifestyle. She chose to focus on the current moment, the present. She decided to be grateful for what exists now, rather than constantly racing toward the next moment and missing out on being present now.

This narrative demonstrates an association between the presence of the concern of death and the change in the flow of time. It indicates the potential relationship between them—in this case, from a future-oriented time perception to encountering the Dasein at any given moment. The authentic condition of embracing the concern of death materialized in slowing down and accepting the finality of life.

An opposite example involved shifting from being stuck in a past-oriented perception—to adopting a more authentic experience of flowing and being in the present. The interviewee, 42 years old, had experienced a crisis in the past that had made him put a total halt to his life. He went to live on his own with no job and nearly no company, cutting himself off from society and living insularly. He spent almost five years in an isolated flat in a remote place, living off a meager state benefit.

His only meaningful connection at the time was with the community's Rabbi. He visited the Rabbi a few times a week to study Torah and for religious teachings. He felt as if his life had frozen and stopped. That way of living gave him a sense of security, feeling that the traumatizing events of his past would never happen again. The frozen time, repeating itself every day with a clear past-facing orientation, provided him with an illusion of invincibility and eternal life.

Then one day—three years before the interview was conducted, the Rabbi collapsed and died of a heart attack. The event was perceived as transformative by the interviewee because, as he reported, suddenly color and movement came back into his life. He abruptly realized that death may occur even in his protected, insular world, and that there is no real protection from it.

This insight accelerated the flowing of time again, and he suddenly started thinking about his situation. He realized that he was still young and had more goals to achieve in life. Gradually, he started looking for a job and participating in family gatherings and social events. All this was led by the realization that life was in the now, in the moment, and that isolation and living in the past, as he had been doing, meant wasting his life away.

Around the time he was interviewed, he started seeing someone romantically and even considered starting a family. Here, too, the authentic condition when facing the concern of death was manifested in completely accepting the finality of life and in being able to live with this reality without attempting to change it.

The heuristic theoretical equation deriving from the above are:
A **"there is no time"** experience, living in constant readiness and activity toward the next moment, is theoretically associated with a neurotic defense of **"there is death"** stance.
A **"there is time"** experience of living at a slow pace and with a past-facing orientation is theoretically associated with a denial defense of invincibility and **"there is no death"** stance.

Analysis of the data suggests that the more individuals experience themselves as living at a fast pace and "having no time" to be in the current moment—the more they may be controlled by a neurotic death anxiety.

Similarly, the more an individual experiences oneself as always trying to stop the rush and ponder at a slow life-pace, the more it is likely that they are controlled by death anxiety. Their denial defense is one of perceived invincibility and an "it won't happen to me" approach. The authentic position when confronting the concern of death is coming to terms with and accepting mortality.

Examples of TLEs related to the dominant experience mode of embodiment, and the concern of freedom:

The following examples are events reported in the study that are related to the dominant experience mode of embodiment. They exemplify its association with the concern of freedom that accompanies this mode of experience.

The first example reveals a physical experience that shifts from a sense of low-impact presence toward a more extended sense of a challenging and authentic self. The interviewee, in her late 40s and a married mother of three children, worked in the tourism industry. She grew up in a very educated and elitist home, in which education and academic degrees were held in high regard. Her parents, both well-known medical doctors in their fields, had pressured her from a very young age to strive for academic achievements as a key to success in life.

She experienced herself as a disappointment when she did not meet the high standards set for her by her parents. She felt her grades were not high enough. She reported always feeling shrunken in her parents' presence, as if she was struggling to breathe. She always felt she was letting them down somehow, that she was never good enough for them.

She thought that throughout most of her childhood she felt shame and guilt for not being a "successful girl". Those emotions always made her feel small and miniscule, regardless of her actual physical size. For her, the experience of being physically diminished was related directly to the sense of responsibility she carried. In her view, her situation was all her fault, because she did not try hard enough. She believed she was—as her parents repeatedly told her—too lazy. We see here how the experience of low-impact physical presence is related to neurotic defensive guilt. It is expressed in taking full responsibility for a situation in order to adress the concern of freedom, as if it were her choice to be lazy.

The interviewee experienced a TLE when at age 25 she won a scholarship to study tourism and the hotel industry in the US. She remembered the first moment she arrived at college and entered her room in the students' dormitories. Suddenly, she felt a huge sense of liberation from her parents' tyranny. She felt she was doing what she really wanted to do, and she felt what she could achieve. She felt joy, relieved from the constant shrinking experience that accompanied her entire adult life until then.

The guilt that was a part of her previous life was reduced, and the interviewee could live her life there, away from her parents, just as she chose to. She was relieved of the constant effort to please them and do what they thought was right. She experienced a period that changed her life. She said that for the first time she felt people were paying attention to her for who she was, rather than relating to her as "the daughter of". Now, she could do whatever she wanted to.

During that time she experienced developing, growing, and expanding her own perception of self and realized how she could fulfill herself. This change toward an expanded presence remained with her when she returned to Israel and started working in tourism independently.

She said that relieving herself from guilt and of the need to prove something to her parents, enabled her to express herself more authentically and independently. Now, she could rely less on others' expectations of her. She felt more confident, and realized she was not responsible for what others might think of her or say to her or how they might respond to her actions and behaviors. Realizing she was not dependent on the responses of others enabled her to gain an increased sense of freedom in her life.

An opposite example involved a shift from a state of a high-impact sense of self-involved vanity and superiority—toward humility and finding the right boundaries. The interviewee, who was in his thirties at the time of the interview, was a 20-year-old conscripted army officer when he experienced a TLE. Prior to it, he used to behave like a tyrant. He always made sure that he clarified to his underlings that he was the only decision-maker around. He never delegated any authority to others, was very strict, and demanded perfection of everyone.

When he was disappointed, he would lash out at people in fits of rage. When he could punish others, he would always go for the severest sanction at hand. He reported that he always felt he had a high-impact presence. He perceived himself as being bigger and mightier than others around him and them as small and scared. This feeling gave him sense of control and calmed him down.

When a mistake or failure occurred, he never took responsibility always found someone else to blame. He would rationalize to himself this was just the way of things. He believed he was born superior; therefore, he deserved things that others were unworthy of.

In other words, by constructing a deterministic world of power relations, the interviewee managed to cancel out any sense of guilt about his actions. He always found justifications for what he had done to others, by thinking "I have no other choice". That is to say, an experience of power and physical size is related, in extreme cases, to abdicating responsibility. This is justified by a denial defense of there being no freedom, because of the false belief of having no choice.

The interviewee's turning point occurred when he walked into the dining hall one day and proceeded to have lunch. At the time, there was an agreement between him and the unit's cook that he would always receive food different from what the other soldiers were served. The interviewee made the cook commit to it because he wanted his underlings to realize that he was more important than they were, as an expression of his need for constant self-aggrandizing.

On that day, a new conscript who was not familiar with the norms at the camp walked into the dining hall. When he witnessed the situation, he stood up and publicly said to the interviewee, "How come we all eat sausages and you are eating chicken?" The incident ended violently, with the interviewee beating up the insolent soldier.

The interviewee's violent outburst shook him deeply. He realized his self-obsession had made him capable of physically hurting others, something he had not done previously. He started realizing that shaking off responsibility and always blaming others was a defense against his concern of freedom. Freedom implied he has responsible for his actions and the choices he could make or avoid making. For the first time in his life, he realized that the choice to assault the other soldier was his responsibility. It was not the soldier's fault, and there was no way he could have justify that behavior to himself or to others.

He started comprehending that all his life he had told himself that he had no choice in order to avoid the guilt that accompanies the sense of freedom. For the first time, he was ready to embark on a journey leading to a more authentic existence. It was a shift toward recognizing his own responsibility for his life, actions, and choices. By relinquishing his previous sense of certainty, he had actually won back his freedom. Now, he could choose how to behave in any event, rather than being "obliged" to think or behave one way or another.

The heuristic theoretical equations deriving from the above are:
An experience of low-impact presence is theoretically associated with a neurotic defense of protective guilt "there is freedom/guilt".
An experience of high impact presence is theoretically associated with responsibility denial defense "there is no freedom/responsibility".

What these cases have in common is that both interviewees found some type of certainty that canceled out their concern of freedom and the uncertainty it evoked. The neurotic defense attributes certainty to an internal locus of control (the interviewee used freedom as an excuse to blame herself, hence canceling out uncertainty). The denial defense attributes certainty to an external locus of control (the interviewee claimed lack of freedom as an excuse to blame others hence canceling out uncertainty). In both cases, gaining back an authentic sense of freedom means relinquishing a false sense of control and assuming responsibility for one's reality.

Examples of TLEs related to the dominant experience mode of relationality and the concern of isolation:

The following examples are events reported in the study that are related to the dominant experience mode of relationality. They exemplify its association with the concern of isolation accompanying this mode of experience.

The first example reveals an experience of relationality that shifts from separateness toward a more authentic experience of belonging. The interviewee, in her thirties, talked about the birth of his first child several years prior to the interview. He said that before his daughter was born, he was used to being in a state of detachment from his social environment. He never got thrilled or excited about anything—not his own birthday or those of other family members. He always felt there was a partition between him and the external world and that no one really knew him or his inner thoughts. Even on his wedding day, he did not manage to feel a sense of thrill.

After the wedding, he moved in with his wife, but he kept feeling separated, as if they were two strangers or roommates sharing a house. The TLE came upon him by surprise, while his wife was giving birth to their first daughter. All of a sudden, when his wife was crying in pain, something broke in him, and he melted. He felt a strong connection to his agonizing wife. He was enraged about not being able to help her, except for helplessly holding her hand. Feelings flooded him with unprecedented intensity, possibly for the first time in his life. When the baby emerged, he felt that "everything is becoming real" and that he had just become a father. For him, the experience was a constituting moment of shifting away from a sense of detachment. He no longer observed himself and others from a safe distance. Now, he could experience tight connections with significant others.

In this narrative, we can see that the interviewee's default position was to keep his feelings to himself, like a lone wolf, and not share them with others. Such behavior may imply the concern of isolation, at the heart of which lies a fear of the pain of being alone and exposed. In other words, the fear that isolation is real is so paralyzing, that people would rather live in solitude. They hide it even from themselves—only to avoid being exposed to this painful truth.

In fact, the moment of his child's birth was a turning point in which the interviewee experienced himself in a more authentic stance. This was when he felt things more strongly and shared those feelings with significant others. Thus, for one moment, the anxiety of exposure and vulnerability dispelled, and the interviewee assumed an authentic position. It was expressed by his ability to share his existential isolation with a close circle of significant others—his daughter and his wife. He managed to create a sense of intimacy among them, in which they share existential isolation. Just as acceptance is the genuine state of the concern of death and responsibility is the authentic state of the concern of freedom, intimacy is the authentic state of the concern of isolation.

An opposite example involved a shift from a condition of extreme symbiosis to an experience of separateness. The interviewee, a 54-years-old woman, talked about her youth, in which she was diagnosed with type 1 diabetes.

The most important thing for the interviewee in her teenage years was to be "just like everybody else". And indeed, until her diagnosis, she managed by her own accord, to "not be different" and not draw any undesired social attention to herself. She said she had put a lot of effort into maintaining her normative image in her social environment. Anything out of the ordinary caused her anxiety, and she took care to hide and conceal it, so that no one would notice the discrepancy.

All that changed once she was diagnosed with diabetes at the age of 16. Now she was different, and there was no way to hide it. More than anything concerning her condition, she remembered her sense of shame for being different. She recalled her difficulty in concealing the effect of the disease on her life, such as the need to inject herself with insulin. Despite all this, she tried to behave as usual and nearly paid for it with her life. She neglected her medical treatment, only to avoid "looking weird".

Only after she turned 20 did she meet a friend who also had diabetes. With her new friend, she managed to discuss her condition in an open and honest way. This relationship brought, for the first time, a sense of intimacy into her life. She realized she could lead a happy life despite being different, because there were people she could intimately share her experience with. She could finally create a deep sense of belonging with others, encompassing all aspects of life.

Here, too, the concern of isolation influenced the interviewee in a way that forced her to put great effort into hiding the difference between her and others. Her goal was to be accepted at all costs. Only after an encounter with a significant other did she manage to find a more balanced position toward the concern of isolation. This new position involved building intimacy and exposing herself to appropriate and willing people.

The heuristic theoretical equations deriving from the above are:
A "there is no other" experience is theoretically associated with a neurotic defense of separateness: "there is isolation".
A "there is another" experience is theoretically associated with a denial defense of merger: "there is no isolation".

As a rule, it can be suggested that the more an individual experiences that there are no others in the world, the more they tend to erect neurotic defenses of isolation and separateness. The more an individual experiences the tangible existence of others, the more they tend to apply isolation-denying defenses through merging with others. The authentic position when facing the concern of isolation is, in both cases—a sense of intimacy and the ability to expose oneself to significant others in a safe and secure manner.

Examples of TLEs related to the dominant experience mode of spatiality, and the concern of meaninglessness:

The following examples are events reported in the study that are related to the predominant experience mode of spatiality. They exemplify its association with the concern of meaninglessness that accompanies this mode of experience.

The first example reveals a shift from spatiality that is too loose and boundaryless (a space that is perceived as chaotic) toward a more authentic, enabling, and protective experience of a space. The interviewee, 30 years old, told us how she joined a sect at about the age of 15. She said the process started when she was about 13 years-old. At the time, she lost interest in school and felt she was living in a chaotic and meaningless environment. She saw friends around her experiment with sex, alcohol, clubbing, and soft drugs. When she tried connecting with them, she felt she was getting lost.

She said her mother and father, who were good and normative parents, were not meaningful role models for her. They did not provide tools to deal with the challenges of growing up or a platform of values to help her construct an internal compass. She described how scornfully she looked upon her friends who engaged in constant grooming. She felt there had to be a greater meaning in life than that. Without clear boundaries, she felt meaninglessness and an inability to place herself in relation to her surroundings.

One day, when she was 15, she met a young man on the beach. From the moment he approached her and started talking about the meaning of life, she felt a powerful connection to him and to all that he represented. He introduced her to his friends, and she soon discovered they were all members of a sect. They obeyed its leader, who ruled it charismatically and authoritatively.

The interviewee was sucked deeply into the sect's life, and she found in the organized and clear existence it offered an appropriate answer to her need for meaning. The sect's life under the leader's command was organized around a radical truth of things that were either allowed or forbidden. It gave the interviewee clear boundaries regarding the realms of "the right life". Within those boundaries, she could find a meaning to her life and feel that she managed to develop and bloom, as she never had before.

In summary, we can learn that the more space is experienced as boundaryless and even chaotic, the more it invokes the anxiety of meaninglessness. It therefore calls for a neurotic defense of finding a clear meaning for life—a radical truth that organizes the space and cancels out the chaotic and boundaryless element in it.

The second example demonstrates the opposite shift, from a space that is too rigid, which also invokes the anxiety of meaninglessness—toward an open space that enables finding meaning. The interviewee, a woman in her fifties, told us about divorcing her first husband 15 years earlier. She said she gotten married when she was very young, to a man many years her senior. He owned a renowned chain of shops and was a successful businessman. She moved into his large house and had everything she could wish for materially.

She raised her children but gradually started feeling uncomfortable in the big house. Indeed, materially she had all she ever wanted, but she felt suffocated, as if she had no space to develop in. Gradually she started feeling as if she were locked in a golden cage.

Regardless of the big house and her luxurious car, she felt that her life had narrowed down. Her world consisted of shopping, raising the children, and idly meeting her friends for coffee at the city center. The shopping excursions, the trips abroad and a hedonistic lifestyle were a defense against the inner experience of an existential vacuum and the anxiety of meaninglessness. In her words, "there was no reason to wake up in the morning".

Gradually, depression developed, and she started taking pills that did not really help. At the heart of her depression was the meaninglessness of her life and her inability to do anything about it. She was afraid of leaving the golden cage that protected her from uncertainty and financial anxiety. Her experience can in fact be described as being trapped in a narrow and suffocating space, which created an existential vacuum. It made her defend herself from it with a self-indulgent life style that denied the emptiness.

The trigger for the divorce was the loss of a beloved friend, who was abruptly killed in a car accident, shortly after the interviewee had met with him in a café. His death shook her profoundly. She said she suddenly realized that she was living in a golden cage and that her life was empty and meaningless.

At 40, she felt half her life was behind her and that she must make sure that the second half would be meaningful. She started a process that aimed to distance her from all that she had previously held dear: a material life of wealth, travel, shopping, and general intemperance.

Only when she distanced herself from the "absolute truth" which tied money to all that mattered in her life did she start to realize that other things could fill her with meaning. The process of rejecting her hedonistic lifestyle involved moving to a more open yet less certain space. This involved a smaller flat, a smaller budget, and a significant decline in her standards of living.

But it was the exposure to a more open space that invited her to experiment with who she really was and to commit to what she was really looking for. Now she embarked on a journey to find what she really wanted to do with her life. She was seeking something that would give her meaning and a feeling that she was helping the environment. In other words, the open space and undoing the hard discipline that previously organized her life (the hedonistic lifestyle) were necessary. It was a condition for her to seek meaning in life at all levels –professionally, romantically, socially, and in terms of her family.

The heuristic theoretical equations deriving from the above are:
An experience of "there is no open/clear space" is theoretically associated with a neurotic defense of order and organization and a need for one radical truth—"there is an order".
An experience of "there is a clear/structured space" is related to a denial defense or existential vacuum and need for a lack of clear meaning: "there is no meaning".

As a rule, it may be suggested that the more one experiences their space as lacking clear boundaries, the more they would seek order and clarity to create meaning in a chaotic world. And the more organized and less enabling the world is, one might sink into an existential vacuum and depression—and respond by seeking disorganization, which lets new possibilities open up.

In both cases, the space blocks finding new possibilities in life, either due to lack of boundaries or due to strict agendas. Hence, it invokes the concern of meaninglessness. In both examples, creating an authentic space—where various possibilities open up—provided a solution to the concern of meaninglessness. It invited the individual to choose their path and be involved in outlining their reality by way of active involvement, rather than as a bystander.

Table 7.2 Heuristic model of association between subjective experience and the implied universal concerns

Neurotic defense (There is anxiety)		*Dominant existential anxiety*	*Denying defense (There is no anxiety)*	
Neurotic defense	*Existential mode of experience*		*Existential mode of experience*	*Denying Defense*
'There is death' Neurotic anxiety, obsession	**'There is no time'** Fast pace, doing	Death and fear of failure and finality	**'There is time'** Slow pace, pondering	**'There is no death'** Invincibility and eternity
'There is freedom/ guilt' Defensive guilt Inner locus of control	**'There is no self'** Low-impact presence	Freedom and fear of guilt	**'There is a self'** High-impact presence	**'There is no guilt/ responsibility'** No guilt, external locus of control
'There is isolation' social isolation, bordering on anti-social	**'There is no other'**, separateness, isolation, lone wolf	Isolation and fear of shame and exposure	**'There are others'** Fusion, team player	**'There is no isolation'** Belonging, conformism
'There is a meaning' A need for clear meaning, inclination toward radicalism	**'There is no clear space'** Open and chaotic space, no social boundaries	Meaninglessness and fear of uncertainty	**'There is a clear space'** Clear law and order, social boundaries	**'There is no meaning'** Inclination toward existential vacuum, nihilism and hedonism

In summary, we present in Table 7.2 the model of theoretical association between the four universal concerns and the four existential modes of experience (Table 7.2).

The "Being-Alongside" Stage of Intervention

This model can be used by the therapist as a roadmap, associating life-world experiences with existential anxieties. Focusing on a dominant aspect of the existential mode of experience provides a meaningful clue as to the dominant existential anxiety in the life of the client in a given context. It is a way to expand the discussion from the experimental phenomenological level described in the previous chapter toward a conversation about the place of existential concerns in the individual's life. Take, for example, an individual whose subjective experience is of fast-paced living that prevents them from experiencing meaningful emotions. It is possible to discuss with them the concern of death and the need to defend oneself from it by constant activity.

Therefore, the conversation will go deeper beyond the experience level to the level of implied existential anxiety. This should enable the client to discover the meaning of this concern and how it is present in their life.

The therapist would use the same methodology of asking phenomenological questions. They would aim to understand the following: How is existential anxiety present? What are the main provinces of meaning in which it is expressed in the client's life? Why is it meaningful for them today? And how does it manifest in various contexts of their life?

We shall now examine the application of these insights for therapeutic intervention as manifested in the second "being alongside" phase of therapy. We shall start from the point we reached at the end of the previous chapter—the modes of clients' lifeworld experiences as described during the phenomenological stage.

Suppose, for example, that a client opts to speak of their relationship as the most disturbing aspect in their life. After examining this province of meaning, we find that regarding the existential modes of experience, the client's most dominant mode of experience is that of relentless activity. They always focus on the next thing: errands, holidays, logistics involving the extended family, the next vacation, the next event. For this client, the dominant mode of experience is a constant racing toward some kind of future. They are unable to be in the present, and they tend to experience prolonged periods of "doing".

Using the above model, we can conclude that for this client, behind the screen lurks the concern of death. They defend themselves from this experience using a neurotic defense of staying in motion and in accelerated action. All this activity shields them from facing the existential concern that is at the heart of the relationship, influencing it.

It is equally possible that in the same context of the client's romantic relationship, the therapist would conclude that the dominant mode of experience is low-impact presence and the constant need to please others. In that case, we would have a meaningful clue that the concern of freedom is behind the screens. Thus, the neurotic defense of diminishing oneself is the way in which the client deals with this concern.

In other cases in the same context, the therapist might come to the conclusion that the dominant mode of experience is symbiosis with their partner. From this, we may conclude using the model, that behind the screens lies the concern of isolation. The denial defense is dominant in the client's life, and dictates the way their distress is experienced.

In yet another case, we might see that the client talks about their distress being connected to a confined space. In other words, the romantic relationship is experienced as if it narrows and limits their options. Here, the client hints toward a denial defense against the concern of meaninglessness. They point toward the need to empty the relationship from its "suffocating" implications, and live in a wider space where "there is choice".

As these examples illustrate, sometimes the same frame (such as a romantic relationship) might indicate different universal concerns for different clients. Clearly, it is important to pay attention to each account in its own rights. Once the client and the therapist figure out together what the dominant mode of experience is in the account (temporality, embodiment, relationality or spatiality), they can capture the universal concern and existential fear behind the screens.

Thus, when the dominant mode of experience is temporality, we can ask about the concern of death and where it meets the client. When the mode of experience is embodiment, we can inquire about the concern of freedom. The same goes for the concerns of isolation and meaninglessness. It is important to note that focusing on these questions should be done sensitively. It must be adjusted to the circumstances and readiness of the client to engage with that content, alongside their awareness of the therapeutic process. This should be done using phenomenological questions aimed at understanding the existential concern as the client experiences it (questions **of what, why and how**).

Here are examples of questions about the concern of death that the therapist can use:

- Tell me about the concern of death in your life. **What** are the most meaningful issues related to this concern?
- **Why** are those issues you raised so significant for you?
- **How** does this meaning manifest itself in your life? Tell me about it in details.

Such questions may be repeated about each of the concerns. It is, of course, possible to explore more than one existential concern in every context (e.g., the concern of death and the concern of freedom). This is relevant if the client reports distress in more than one dominant mode of experience. The goal at this point is to discuss the relevant existential concern for the client and make them aware of how these concerns affects their life.

Note that it is not necessary to go deeply into all of the concerns. It is important to delve into those where the client views themself as less adjusted—the ones more influential over their life. Even one concern that is chosen as significant for the client can enable the therapist to "be alongside" them. This stage will pave the way for the next and last stage of therapy.

It is also vital to recognize that exploring the client's universal concerns requires a great deal of time and constitutes the main part of all branches of existential therapy. Therefore, a patient and dynamic approach is needed in order to identify the presence of concerns in different aspects of the client's life. The deeper the exploration—the easier it will be to move on toward the last stage of therapy.

To summarize this chapter, the suggested theoretical model assists in deepening the conversation from the experience-based context-dependent level in which it had taken place initially. Now, it moves toward a more profound layer, dealing with the existential concerns at the heart of the client's subjective experience. It means "being-alongside" the client in their encounter with existential anxiety. Based on raising the client's awareness of the existential concern reflected by their subjective experience, it is possible to help them "be differently". In other words, expanding their situational freedom enables a change in the way they experience their life, as explored in the next and final chapter.

Reference

Davidov, J., & Russo-Netzer, P. (2021). Exploring the phenomenological structure of existential anxiety as lived through transformative life experiences. *Anxiety, Stress, & Coping*, 1–16.

CHAPTER 8

Being Otherwise—Therapeutic Paths, Therapeutic Partnership and the Existential Authenticity Model

Abstract This chapter introduces existential authenticity as the central concept to guide the psychotherapeutic process in order to enable individuals to achieve a balanced experience of existential anxiety, as a journey "from forgetfulness of being to mindfulness of being." Confronting and balancing existential anxiety in an authentic manner may help clients accept the challenge of responsibility for their own existence and transform anxieties into virtues—including acceptance of the finality of death, development of intimacy and love, and the co-discovery of meaning. The systematic approach presented in this book offers practical steps that may bridge the gap between subjective experience and the notion of existential anxiety, making intervention and clinical work with this concept more accessible.

Keywords Existential authenticity model • Acceptance of the finality of death • Assuming responsibility • Intimacy and love • Co-discovery of meaning

Interventions based on the existential approach are not referred to as 'therapeutic counseling' but rather as 'therapeutic relationship' (Spinelli, 2002). This is not a relationship between equals—as one of them seeks help and the other attempts to provide it. However, there will be no useful work if mutual meaning is not created between the two. The client is at

J. Davidov, P. Russo-Netzer, *Existential Authenticity*,
https://doi.org/10.1007/978-3-031-07842-2_8

the center of therapy, and uses the conversation to find a new perspective from which to observe his or her life. The therapist is seen as a partner who accompanies the client in their search for meaning and authentic way of being in the world. Together they aim to capture the client's inner experience and its underlying existential concerns.

As discussed, the **first stage** of this process is phenomenological ('being for'), because through active listening the therapist tries to get as close as possible to the client's experience and subjective world. This work also enables the clients to examine their own 'taken for granted' perception of self and reality. It prepares them to view their current life as one possibility among many they can choose from in the given circumstances. Here, the main 'themes' or patterns constructing the client's experience can be identified. Also important to this stage is that the therapists can evaluate the ways in which their clients choose to express their narratives and to better understand 'what it is like to be the client' (i.e. to identify the modes of their lifeworld experience).

At the **second stage** the therapist tries to 'capture' and establish insights regarding the universal concerns relevant to the client's experience. This is the stage of 'being with', in which the the focus of the process is on learning how those concerns influence and effect the client's lifeworld.

The purpose of the **third** stage is to expose the client to other ways of living. At the heart of this stage is a combination of the types of knowledge crystallized in previous stages. The main 'themes' and patterns in the client's day-to-day experience (identified in the first stage) are now explored in light of the universal concerns that are implied in them (identified in the second stage). Based on these insights, the goal of the third stage is to regulate the existential concerns and to enable the client to gain a greater degree of situational freedom in which they can choose their own way of experiencing reality. In other words, the purpose of this stage is to increase the client's sense of existential authenticity and to enhance their freedom to construct their life in a way that is meaningful for them.

This chapter presents the model of existential authenticity and explores the possible paths of regulating each existential concern.

Existential Authenticity Model

As discussed, there are four paths that may lead an individual from a state of 'forgetfulness of being' or automatic behavior patterns, toward an authentic consciousness aware of different ways of being. The following summarizing table presents recommended path for each of the identified universal concerns. It should be noted that this table is advisory. It is flexible in adjustment to the client's needs and the therapeutic progress. It aims to give general guidelines and directions, yet therapists should always bear in mind the importance of sensitivity, openness, and flexibility throughout the process (See Table 8.1).

The general focus at this point in therapy is increasing the client's capacity to bear a direct, experience-based contact with their existential concerns.

Table 8.1 The existential authenticity model

Existential mode of experience	*Existential Concern*	*Range of Psychological defenses*	*Therapeutic Path*	*Therapeutic goal: The Authentic Condition*
Temporality Between action and fast pace living to pondering and slow pace	Death and fear of finality and failure	*Between obsessive neurosis to illusion of invulnerability*	*Being anxious to the right extent:* **being now, thought and action combined**	Accepting finality, coming to terms with change
Embodiment Between low-impact and high-impact presence	Freedom and fear of guilt	Between defensive guilt to denying responsibility	*Feeling guilty to the right extent:* **Being present, flexibility and changing**	Assuming responsibility
Relationality: Between 'lone wolf' and 'team player'	Isolation and fear of shame and exposure	*Between conformism to a-social position*	*Being exposed to the right extent:* **Being together, partnership between equals**	Creating intimacy and sense of belongingness
Spatiality: Between chaotic loose boundaries and strict social and material boundaries	Meaninglessness and fear of uncertainty	*Between radicalism and control to existential vacuum*	*Living with doubt, striving to collaboration and commitment to a given social context:* **Being here, commitment to lived context**	Co-discovery of meaning

For example, consider a case in which the dominant concern the client reports on in a certain context (i.e., work, romantic relationship, etc.) is the concern of death. The suggested theoretical model enables the therapist to help the client to regulate their experience of this concern to better cope with potential tension and distress that might accompany it. There are two ways to such intervention—either through direct focus on the client's lived experience of the concern of death, or cognitively working with patterns and conceptualization associated with this concern. The first way—the experiential one—aims to help the clients to experience their here-and-now through regulating their lived experience of the rhythm of time (e.g. slowing down a fast pace to influence neurotic oriented defenses, or accelerating a slow pace in order to influence denial oriented defenses).

The second one—the more cognitive approach—is targeted towards the anxiety related to death concern (i.e., fear of finality and failure) in order to help the clients to contain it and reduce its affect over their experience. In this context, the more the client can contain their fear of failure and finality triggered by the death concern, the more they can accept their own experience of being vulnerable and finite (the authentic position). This, in turn, would enable them to regulate their rhythm in life and enhance situational freedom in a given context.

Case Study

Danny, in his 30s, was used to living most of his life in an accelerated pace, always seeking for the next exciting challenge and feeling as if he can achieve whatever he wants in life. Several years before turning to counseling, Danny experienced a traumatic event when he found the body of his best friend who committed suicide. Following this event Danny started to think of his own death and finality, and consequently began having panic attacks and anxiety that caused a lot of distress in his life. Nevertheless, Danny continued his fast paced life, trying to maintain the same level of hectic activity he used to have before the traumatic event occurred. In accordance with the existential authenticity approach and after it became clear that Danny is being managed by the universal concern of death, a therapeutic path was suggested to enable him to regulate his fast paced life on the one hand, and to come to terms with his physical and emotional boundaries and limitations on the other hand. Danny was advised to become more attuned to his experiences in the here and now, focusing on day-to say activities that gave him a sense of security and stability such as family and work, while calming down the need to look for adventures and unexpected surprises. When the pace in his life slowed down, Danny could contain the thought that there are limitations to his power, and that he was vulnerable (the authentic stance regarding the concern of death). This cleared the path to explore what is meaningful to him in his life. Danny realized at that point that the most prominent goal in his life is to find a spouse and to start his own family. This goal required him to step outside his 'comfort zone' and to challenge himself, but this time not for the sake of adventure and extreme lifestyle but for a meaningful cause that he identified as helpful despite the risk of experiencing anxiety or new panic attacks. By confronting his concern of death and being able to accept and contain it (i.e., the authentic stance), Danny could better identify what is meaningful to him in his life, and to follow it. As he later found out, following what is meaningful to him led to reduced, and even the disappearance of his panic attacks, as he was able to remind himself at each point why he chose to engage with an activity and how it was meaningful to him.

The specific methods for adjusting and regulating the pace of life and attitude towards the concern of death may vary to suit the therapist's available toolbox. For example, cognitive tools of stress management, effective moderation, mindfulness or cognitive coping could be used here. Alternatively, more dynamic techniques, which encourage emotional connection to an adequate life tempo, could also be applied. Regardless of the available toolkit, the goal remains the same—changing the attitude toward the concern of death, both in terms of cognitive perception and experientially. This would enable the client to get closer to an **authentic position of acceptance** of **and coming to terms with finality, failure, and eventually death**. It would also constitute an ability to live with some degree of death concern without attempting to apply neurotic or denial oriented defenses, which might invoke distress.

If, in another case, the dominant concern is that of freedom, then the client and the therapist should examine other ways for the client to live with the anxiety of guilt that characterizes this concern. This should be done according to the relevant context, for example their work, relationship, and so on. In such a case, the therapist and client could explore how to regulate their concern of freedom in the reality of the client's life through the two domains of the authenticity model: regulating the embodiment subjective experience on the one hand, and regulating the cognitive perception of guilt on the other hand.

Either way, a more authentic stance toward life can be established. The more the client can change their cognitive relation to the concern of freedom and contain their fear of guilt, the more they can influence their experience of presence in various contexts, and vice versa. The specific methods used here may include a variety of practices such as techniques encouraging an extended presence characterized by body language and open behavioral position. Or, on the other hand, techniques aiming to make rigid thought and behavior more flexible may be used as well. In either case, the goal is the same—the more an individual can regulate and modify their relationship with the concern of freedom, **the more they can assume responsibility over their experience** (the authentic position). This type of work may reduce their distress in the relevant situation.

In a third case, if the dominant concern is isolation, we can explore how to increase the levels of the client's authenticity through this path. Here too we can use either experiential or cognitive methods to influence and to regulate the concern of isolation.

From an experiential point of view, directly working on opening up and being exposed in front of others can be used to relieve a rigid sense of isolation and fear of exposure. Or, on the other hand, exploring what makes the client unique may be used to break out of a tendency to over-merge with the other in order to gain recognition or validation. Modifying the concern of isolation can also be applied cognitively by helping clients to contain and regulate their fear of exposure and sense of shame worthlessness. Regulating the clients' perception of their concern of isolation may positively affect their relationships with others.

The more one can experience their relationships with others in a more exposed and open manner, the more they can increase their **sense of intimacy and ability to constitute partnerships between equals** (the authentic position when facing the concern of isolation). This would help reduce their distress in relevant situations.

Case study
Orit, in her 40s, suffered from eating disorder that caused her much shame, and led her to hide this behavior from her husband, children and best friends. She found different creative ways to hide this behavior from others, but kept feeling shame and disgust, with a tendency to self-denial and putting other people's needs before her own because she believed herself to be 'not an important person'. She never dared to look for a job because she felt unworthy and inferior, stating that to be a housewife was all that she could really do. Through the therapeutic process, the universal concern of isolation and the sense of shame associated with exposure were identified. Consequently, a therapeutic path could be planned to help her to regulate her ability to contain rejection and overcome her fear of losing other people. This paved the way for her to realize that what she really wanted was to develop a professional career in the field of special education. The work-related goal only appeared after Orit could endure and contain exposure to her needs without being overwhelmed with shame (the authentic stance). Thus, by regulating the universal concern of isolation and the subsequent fear of exposure and shame, the client could find what is meaningful in her life and follow it. The more she dared to follow what is meaningful, the less she suffered from her eating disorder later on.

Case Study
Amit, in his 30s, always felt alienated from his social surroundings. Amit was multi-talented and had major achievements in various fields he engaged in. However, after a certain period of being involved in some activity he began feeling drained and lost interest, along with a need to move on to the 'next thing'. According to him, this pattern made him feel alienated from his social environment, and caused ongoing distress that eventually led him to therapy. Amit's main complaint was that he experienced a feeling of emptiness accompanied by depression. In the therapeutic process, Amit gradually learned to identify the worry of meaninglessness that was involved in his experience, which was stemming from not being able to commit

himself to a given context and the fear of uncertainty that accompanied it. Amit gradually learned to identify the exact moment in which an occupation, hobby or a relationship lost its appeal to him, and realized that this experience reflects an encounter with doubt and uncertainty that he couldn't contain, and so he fled to the next thing. Through the therapeutic process, he learned to contain this uncertainty long enough (the authentic stance) to rediscover the lost sense of meaning, and to commit to his experience. This commitment has led Amit to the re-discovering meaning, and thus meaning could be anchored in a specific given context.

And, if the main universal concern is that of meaninglessness and the associated fear of uncertainty, we can help the client examine how to increase his or her authenticity through the path of seeking meaning. The more the individual can experience his spatiality in a more flexible and creative way, the more they can strive toward active partnership and make a commitment with their environment. In addition, the more a client can contain uncertainty and doubt, the more he or she can regulate their sense of meaninglessness. Regulating meaninglessness can facilitate the conditions to achieving a more **authentic way of living, and to enable co-discovery of meaning in life and social surroundings**.

Case Study

Michal, in her 50s, reported high levels of distress when she engaged in assertive behavior with other people or expressed her opinion out loud. When the therapist explored more closely this distress, it was found that it contained guilt and self-anger that erupted whenever the Michal wanted to influence others in any way. She always felt that she should keep a low profile and low-impact presence, and whenever she 'failed' to to do so she was filled with increased levels of guilt for 'taking someone else's place', and found herself very apologetic toward others. As the process progressed, it became clear that this guilt was related to a lived experience of her mom, whom Michal perceived to be a repressive person, which led her to develop anxiety around the universal concern of freedom. When Michal learned to contain this guilt, while understanding that being assertive didn't mean that she was repressive (the authentic stance), and could gradually better observe what is meaningful to her in her life—to speak out, to make a difference, to have an impact and influence people, and to give voice to her values. In other words, by regulating the existential concern of freedom and guilt, Michal could realize her values in various social contexts and surroundings. She could then direct her life toward the goal of being more present and confident while being in the company of other people, and to assume responsibility over her behavior.

In summary, existential authenticity constitutes a therapeutic path in which the therapist explores with the client the right dose of existential anxiety they can allow into their life. Too much of it might invoke distracting neurotic or denial-oriented defenses, which in turn may cause suffering and distress. The authentic response is both experience and perception based.

In its experience-based it works through influencing the four modes of experience—the tempo of life, the physical experience of 'self' and the 'I', the relationships with others, and the felt experience of space. In its perception or cognitive based, it works through containing the fear and anxieties embedded in the four existential concerns of death, freedom, isolation, and meaninglessness.

The work on the four existential modes of experience on the one hand and regulating the cognitive perception of the four existential concerns on the other hand have the power to generate an essential change in the way individuals experience themselves and their reality. The authentic response may transform the energy embodied in existential anxiety toward a life that involves accepting and coming to terms with death; being able to take responsibility; sharing intimacy with significant others; and invoking a sense of active participation and shared discovery of meaning in life. These four virtues may express the gift of existential authenticity, and offer individuals who follow such path an increased degree of situational freedom, a more holistic experience of well-being, and meaning in life.

To conclude, the following flowchart illustrates a suggested working model of the existential authenticity approach. Although presented in a linear form, it should be considered as representing a holistic process that requires nuanced and sensitive and flexible approach, open to adaptations for different individuals' needs, concerns and goals (See Fig. 8.1).

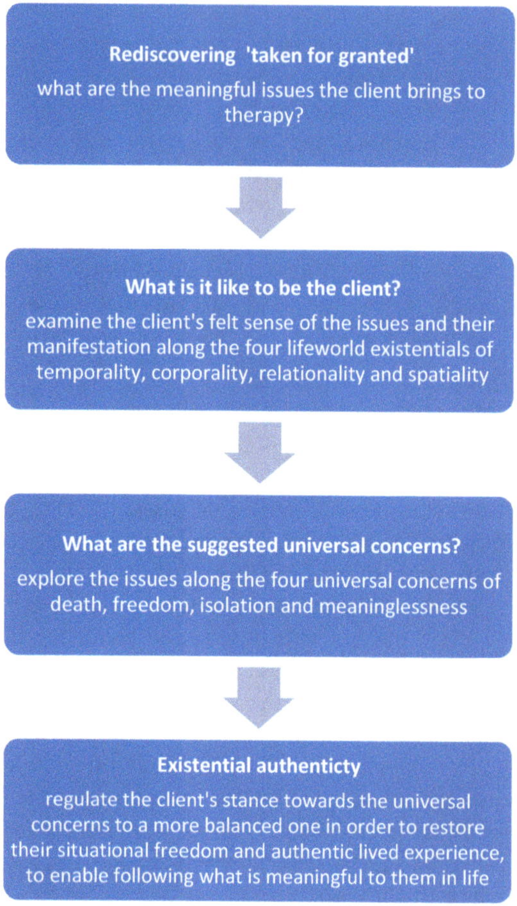

Fig. 8.1 Existential Authenticity working model flowchart

Reference

Spinelli, E. (2002). The therapeutic relationship as viewed by existential psychotherapy: Re-embracing the world. *Journal of Contemporary Psychotherapy*, 32(1), 111–118. https://doi-org.ezproxy.haifa.ac.il/10.1023/A:1015547632139

Epilogue

The human search for freedom and meaning throughout history traces back to ancient tales and myths in different cultures and traditions around the globe, such as religions (e.g. exodus), mythologies (e.g. Greek mythology, Gilgamesh epic), and modern literature the stories (e.g. the Wizard of Oz, Lord of the Rings, to name a few). In all these instances, the human longing for answers concerning the four existential focal points for mankind—death, freedom, isolation, and meaning—is evident. The journey is often characterized by instability, uncertainty, and the limitation of human existence. Such vulnerability that may sometimes be challenging and painful is also at the heart of existential authenticity, and as such, it may enable vitality and more holistic experience of life, with all its shades and colors.

By listening closely to people's accounts of their experience through the lifeworld existentials involved (i.e. temporality, spatiality, embodiment, and relationality), we can derive valuable information regarding the manner in which the client constructs their reality. Taking the time to understand the client's lived experience more fully may allow to discern deep-seated values and to discover new possibilities and ways to live differently and more meaningfully. Based on this foundation, therapists will be more capable of assisting clients in translating their values into practical activity in their everyday life. Prioritizing meaning (Russo-Netzer, 2018)—expressed in our day-to-day choices of investing our time and energy resources—was found to be connected with happiness, life satisfaction,

J. Davidov, P. Russo-Netzer, *Existential Authenticity*,
https://doi.org/10.1007/978-3-031-07842-2

and gratitude among adults. This suggests that focusing on and prioritizing engagement with activities that are inherently value-congruent may serve as a tangible and concrete mechanism for instilling life with meaning and increasing authenticity.

This book explored key fundamentals of existential thought with a special focus on authenticity along with potential pathways to nurture it in everyday life and as part of psychotherapeutic interventions. Viewed as a human response to the universal givens, authenticity involves embracing discomfort, flexibility, and the courage required to confront and leverage anxiety towards attaining a more integrative way of being in the world. The 'road map' presented in this book offers a possible re-organization of this approach to authenticity in order make it more accessible for clinical use. Rather than a diagnostic method, it is a dynamic, process-based approach to a more authentic and balanced way of living. Such a 'road-map' may be especially relevant in a postmodern society, in which a multiplicity of choices and relativism prevail, to provide the individual with an anchor and a potential compass to navigate their way through the uncertainties, and ambiguity of current human condition. The purpose of the book is to help individuals explore new possibilities that stretch beyond their comfort zone, and to embark on a journey to an unknown landscape of life following that which is meaningful and authentic for them. Such a journey is challenging as it brings people into direct contact with their existential anxiety, but it also offers new opportunities and possibilities to live life to the fullest. Facing life's gravity and beauty requires taking action, intentionality, responsibility and courage, or in different words—being existentially authentic!

Reference

Russo-Netzer, P. (2018). Prioritizing meaning as a pathway to meaning in life and general well-being. Journal of Happiness Studies, 20(6), 1863–1891. https://doi.org/10.1007/s10902-018-0031-y

Index

J. Davidov, P. Russo-Netzer, *Existential Authenticity*,
https://doi.org/10.1007/978-3-031-07842-2

FSC
www.fsc.org
MIX
Papier | Fördert gute Waldnutzung
FSC® C083411

Kolibri 360 GmbH
Ferdinand-Jühlke-Straße 7
99095 Erfurt, Deutschland
produktsicherheit@kolibri360.de